OVERVIEW

Overview

Do you sometimes feel that your professional style is too passive, too hesitant and weak? Or do you find yourself acting aggressively toward others in the workplace, being too critical and overbearing?

Do you wonder if there is another professional business style that might be right for you? The answer may well be yes. Many people find that an assertive style meets their professional needs. Others around you appreciate this solid, constructive approach. And you can feel in control using this style to deal with co-workers or even manage or supervise employees. The assertive style can be your win-win style.

Try the role of an assertive business professional. It can be the right style for you. You can find yourself acting proactively and dealing with others responsibly. What a great feeling. The good news is that you don't have to achieve this role by yourself. This course will give you tools to help. You will learn about:

- becoming an assertive professional,

- proactive listening strategies,
- constructive feedback strategies.

Do you sometimes feel trapped in the way you commonly act at work? Or even angry at others who act as though you're a nonentity or someone to be avoided?

How would you like to take the lead in developing the assertive professional style you've dreamed of having, one that lets you avoid traps and anger? It's up to you to decide when you want to take charge of your life.

You've reached the right conclusion when you decide that you're the best person to take the lead in developing your professional style. You can blossom as an individual when your actions form the foundation for an assertive style that you can build on and strengthen.

Your self-confidence will increase as you use the course's methods and guidelines to change your professional style to the style you've dreamed of having.

If you have an optimistic attitude, your efforts to develop your style can be both personally and professionally rewarding. The material covered in this course will give you the tools to help yourself. The three lessons are:

- Developing Your Assertive Style,
- Self-development Strategies,
- Assertive Interactions.

CHAPTER I - ASSERTING YOURSELF PROFESSIONALLY

CHAPTER I - Asserting Yourself Professionally
SECTION I - Becoming an Assertive Professional
SECTION II - Proactive Listening Strategies
SECTION III - Constructive Feedback Strategy

SECTION I - BECOMING AN ASSERTIVE PROFESSIONAL

SECTION I - Becoming an Assertive Professional

In this section, you'll learn questions to ask, methods to employ, and guidelines to follow to become an assertive business professional. You'll learn about:
- determining your professional style,
- achieving your assertiveness goal, and
- modifying your professional style.

STRATEGIES FOR BECOMING AN ASSERTIVE BUSINESS PROFESSIONAL

Strategies for becoming an assertive business professional

"In calm water every ship has a good captain." -- Swedish proverb

Question

Do you know someone with a confident, assertive style that enables him to be a good captain in any business setting, whether the situation is calm or stormy? Do you envy his ability? Do you think the following statement is true or false?

Any person can master the assertive professional style with the proper attitude and effort.

Options

1. true
2. false

Answers

Actually, there's no secret involved, and no magic. By following the designated change strategies, you can learn to be professionally assertive.

Option 1: This statement is true. By applying certain strategies, like proactive listening and constructive feedback, any person can exhibit an assertive style.

Option 2: This statement is not false. There are strategies available that any person can apply to change their behavior toward a more assertive style.

You've decided there's reason to evaluate your professional style. After all, it's never too late to learn and to improve your current abilities and skills.

Self-evaluate

"I did some self-evaluation and talked with a few peers. I was surprised to find how aggressive my style was. Time to change? You bet."

Plan change

"Change doesn't just happen. You have to plan to make it happen. I now have a specific plan to develop a more assertive style."

Evaluating your current style may prompt a desire to change it. If so, plan how to implement necessary change. Use change strategies to work toward your goal of becoming an assertive professional. Both you and your co-workers or staff will benefit once you've implemented the strategies and reaped the rewards of becoming professionally assertive. The benefits of using change strategies are:

- improving your self-image,
- enhancing your leadership ability,
- reducing your stress,
- improving relations with others.

Question

Assertive Communication

Based on what you've learned, what are benefits of learning change strategies to apply to your professional style?

Options
1. You can probably lower stress and feel more relaxed.
2. You can avoid negative interactions with others.
3. You can enhance your ability to act as a leader.
4. You can see improvement in relations with others.
5. You can see an improvement in your self-image.

Answer

Actually, all but one of these statements reflect the benefits of learning change strategies for changing your professional style. Avoiding negative interactions is not a specified benefit.

Option 1: This is a correct choice. Lowering stress benefits you by contributing to your overall mental and physical health and makes you somebody others enjoy being around.

Option 2: This choice is incorrect. Avoidance is not a benefit to you or your co-workers. In fact, you will still need to tackle those possibly negative interactions. Using change strategies can help you make these interactions positive.

Option 3: This choice is correct. By choosing to change your professional style to one that's more assertive, you enhance your ability to lead because people will respond more positively to your input.

Option 4: Correct. If you are choosing to change, this means that you have recognized a need to change perhaps based on peer feedback. By applying change strategies to your professional style, you will benefit by improving your relations with others.

Sorin Dumitrascu

Option 5: Correct. By learning strategies for changing your professional style, you are investing in yourself and seeking to improve yourself. This will help you feel better about yourself and your interactions with others, thus improving your self-image.

DETERMINING PERSONAL PROFESSIONAL STYLE

Determining personal professional style

Have you ever thought life at work would be immeasurably better if you had a formula for the perfect professional style? Actually, there are methods that can help you investigate your current style and change it if you so choose.

In this topic, you'll learn the definition of professional style and the questions to ask to determine your current style. You'll learn about:
- defining professional style,
- questions to ask to determine your style.

Your professional style is the way you conduct yourself as you interact with co-workers or subordinates in the workplace. What is your current professional style--aggressive, passive, assertive? It's important that you identify the style you use on a daily basis. This definition gives you a baseline to work from as you decide if, or how, you want to change your professional business style. From this baseline, you can define the changes and improvements that you want to make in your style.

You've defined professional style and you're ready to undertake a review of your own style. You're ready to begin asking questions to determine your current style.

Launegayer's Observation--"Asking dumb questions is easier than correcting dumb mistakes"--is worth noting here. Your task is to ask questions. The answers will help you avoid future professional mistakes.

The traits of an assertive professional style can be your guide for asking questions. Answers will help you pinpoint whether you're assertive. The first question--"Do I use proactive listening strategies?"--helps you determine how effective you are at connecting with and gathering information from others.

Beginning of the meeting

Judith makes it a point to clarify the reason for a meeting before conversation begins. That's an important element of a proactive listening strategy.

End of the meeting

Aaron always summarizes the main points of a discussion and the decisions reached by the participants-- an important element of the proactive listening strategy.

Both Judith and Aaron use a proactive listening strategy, a trait of an assertive business professional. You'll find that this strategy involves actions other than just listening passively to someone. The second question--"Do I use constructive feedback strategies?"--helps you determine how effective you are at connecting with others and providing helpful, useful information.

For example, you're providing constructive feedback when you suggest to a team leader that meetings can be

Assertive Communication

run more effectively or when you present an idea for improving how meetings are structured and conducted.

Question

A constructive feedback strategy employs both positive feedback and constructive criticism. Your use of this strategy fosters growth and improvement in the people receiving your ideas and suggestions.

Examine your own behavior during a recent situation in which you provided feedback to a co-worker or employee. Do you think you provided constructive feedback?

Options

1. no
2. very little
3. unsure
4. to some extent
5. yes

Answers

Regardless of your current level of use of constructive feedback, you can benefit from further developing your skills in this area.

Question

You're ready to discover where you stand on the professional-style continuum. Which questions would you ask to determine your current professional style?

Options

1. How well do I delegate tasks to others?
2. Do I complete assignments in the correct order?
3. How well do I provide useful feedback to others?
4. Am I proactive when I listen to others?

Answer

Actually, you need to ask if you provide constructive feedback and listen proactively in order to determine your professional style.

Option 1: This choice is incorrect. This question does not help you understand how you connect or communicate with others. Rather, it assesses your project management skills.

Option 2: This is an incorrect choice. This question does not help you understand how you connect or communicate with others because it only assesses your work habits.

Option 3: This is a correct choice. This question helps you determine how effective you are at connecting with others and providing them helpful, useful information.

Option 4: This choice is correct. This question helps you determine how effective you are at connecting with and gathering information from others.

Ask yourself if you use proactive listening strategies and constructive feedback strategies. What do the answers tell you? If your style is too passive, you may realize you're being taken advantage of. If your style is aggressive, others may resent or fear you. The answers to the questions may indicate that you need to develop a more assertive professional style. If that's the case, continue the course for help cultivating the assertive style you want to own and use.

Have you decided you need to improve your professional style? In this topic, you learned the definition of professional style. You also learned to ask these questions to help you determine your current professional business style:

- Do I frequently use proactive listening strategies?

Assertive Communication

- Am I using constructive feedback strategies?

ACHIEVING AN ASSERTIVE PROFESSIONAL GOAL

Achieving an assertive professional goal

Setting life goals has been stressed in popular literature in recent years. What goals have you set for yourself as a business professional?

Question

Perhaps you've set a goal to become professionally assertive. Consider this statement:

You're unwise to set goals because you'll never keep them or attain them.

Options

1. strongly disagree
2. disagree
3. unsure
4. agree
5. strongly agree

Answer

Goals are attainable if they are realistic and if you follow well- established methods to achieve them.

Assertive Communication

When you set a goal to be an assertive professional, you're actually acting assertively. It's an action that supports the style you want to adopt. Once you establish your goal, you're ready to take actions to become more assertive.

In this topic, you'll learn about three common methods of achieving the goal of being an assertive professional. In pursuit of your goal, you'll learn about:
- acting supportively,
- acting proactively,
- acting fairly.

Stop and reflect for a moment. Are you supportive of others in the workplace--your co-workers or employees? Do you want to be supportive?

Carl is a senior manager in a large suburban bank. Carl's actions illustrate the first method you can use to become an assertive professional: acting supportively toward others.

supporting other managers

"I enjoy mentoring the new managers. I share my experiences and expertise to help them grow and avoid the mistakes I made as a new manager."

supporting staff

"I support my staff by ensuring that they receive the training they request or that I believe would benefit them. I'm a strong believer in growth through training."

Carl knows that his supportive actions on behalf of employees can increase their morale as he helps them reach their potential. He knows they appreciate his assertive support.

The second method to use is to act proactively toward others in the workplace.

You're proactive when you forcefully take the lead. You identify and address issues before they become problems. You address questions before others become concerned about them. Your proactive approach can increase other employees' self-confidence.

Look for issues

"I always ask others on the team if there are issues we're missing as we move forward on the project. I help ensure that there are no hidden issues."

Address issues

"If I hear of any questions raised by staff, I make it a point to address them immediately. I stop a lot of small issues from becoming concerns this way."

The third method to become an assertive professional is to act fairly toward others. This method flows logically from its two companion methods. From a professional viewpoint, acting fairly is being open and direct with others and being nonjudgmental. Others will definitely take notice when you add this method to your professional style.

Be open and direct

"It's important to me to be fair to everyone--peers and employees alike. I can be open and direct because people know I don't try to deceive and I don't have favorites. I think I gain a lot of respect for my emphasis on fairness in the workplace."

Be nonjudgmental

"I try not to label people. I work at being objective and making observations rather than up front judgments. A nonjudgmental approach pays dividends in the workplace."

Assertive Communication

Others in the workplace will have a positive response to your supportive professional style because everyone appreciates being dealt with fairly.

Question

Based on what you've learned, match each method for achieving an assertive professional goal with the corresponding statement.

Options

A. acting supportively
B. acting proactively
C. acting fairly

Targets

1. I suggest you attend the supervisory skills course.
2. I'd like to identify issues we might face on the new project.
3. I don't want to judge the issue before we discuss it.

Answers

In fact, the correct answers are indicated above. It's important to understand how to use the methods taught in this topic to achieve your assertiveness goal.

Suggesting further development to an employee is a way of providing support for that person. It can increase employees' morale as you help them reach their potential.

By assessing potential problems before they arise, you are being proactive and keeping the focus positive. By not being proactive, you may miss opportunities or create a situation for a difficult encounter in the future.

Suspending judgment on a matter or decision allows you to be fair to all persons involved. You can obtain the employee's opinion or the team's feedback and work together on a solution before it becomes a real problem.

You may feel more effective and self-assured as you begin to use the methods for achieving your assertiveness goal. There are important methods to put into practice as you begin the process of becoming more assertive. When you act in a supportive, proactive, and fair manner, others in the workplace will take notice. And you will undoubtedly be glad you made the concerted effort to achieve your assertiveness goal as you gain others' recognition and respect.

GUIDELINES FOR MODIFYING A PROFESSIONAL STYLE

Guidelines for modifying a professional style

If you've identified your style, set your goal, and clarified methods for achieving your goal, you're on your way to a change that will be professionally rewarding. If you've decided you want to change to an assertive style, there are some guidelines that can help you.

It's important to realize that even if you exhibit some of the attributes of an assertive business professional now, you can always improve and strengthen them.

In this topic, you'll learn about three guidelines for modifying your current professional style. They are:
- acknowledging the desire to change,
- planning your change,
- implementing your plan.

The first guideline is very straightforward and probably seems obvious, but it isn't always followed in everyday practice. First, you need to actually acknowledge your desire to change. That includes owning the desire and being able to articulate the benefits you can gain by becoming an assertive business professional.

I can avoid problems

"I'm tired of constantly reacting to situations. I want to be proactive and resolve employee issues before they become problems. That would be a relief for everyone."

I can be positive

"I'd like to take a positive approach in giving feedback and assessments. And I'd like to give constructive criticism when needed to address negative issues."

Proactive, positive, and constructive are all traits that you might like to acquire by changing and improving your professional style.

The second guideline you'd do well to follow is to plan your change. It's not a radical idea, but it's surprising how many people set a goal and immediately charge off to achieve it. In their haste, they fail to lay out a clear plan on how to get where they want to go. Often they don't set a deadline for reaching their goal or even identify how they'll know if the goal, or a milestone along the way, is actually achieved.

Planning your goal is done through a series of steps.

State the goal.

State your goal in clear, concise terms that another professional can readily understand. Ensure that the goal is stated in terms that can be observed and measured. For example, increase one-on-one meetings with all staff members to once per month.

Identify the action steps.

Clearly identify the action steps required to move toward your goal. The completion of a step can constitute a milestone reached. Action steps should be observable and measurable. For example, one step could be to complete the assessment plan by month's end.

Set a timetable.

It's important to establish a timetable for achieving your action steps and final goal. Specify a date to complete each step, and put the information on a chart you can use to track your progress toward your goal. If you miss a date, revise your plan and timetable as necessary.

Plan your self-assessments.

Finally, you will want to plan points where you do self-assessments. The completion of an action step or milestone is a good time for this activity. This is when you ask yourself how you're doing in keeping to your timetable and completing your action steps.

Question

Based on what you've just learned, how should you go about planning your change in professional style?

Options

1. I should specify actions needed to reach my goal.
2. I need to have the right staff support in place.
3. I have to know how to assess my progress.
4. I need to state my desire for change as a goal.
5. I should know the timetable I'm working with.

Answers

Actually, the planning necessary to ensure progress requires stating the goal and action steps, setting a timetable, and completing assessments.

$t.getLocalizedString("transcript.option") 1: This choice is correct. By specifying actions to reach your goal, you are laying out a clear plan that can be understood and measured.

$t.getLocalizedString("transcript.option") 2: Incorrect. Having support staff is not one of the steps in planning for change in your professional style. The nature of any support staff may be beyond your control. Strategies for planning your change are activities fully within your control.

$t.getLocalizedString("transcript.option") 3: This is a correct choice. To gauge whether you have made satisfactory progress, you need to be able to assess your goals. This means they must be measurable and attached to a clear timeline.

$t.getLocalizedString("transcript.option") 4: This is a correct choice. By stating your desire to change as a goal, you lay out a clear plan for getting where you want to go. You should state your goal in clear, concise terms to make it readily understood by another professional.

$t.getLocalizedString("transcript.option") 5: Correct. By establishing a timetable, you can track your progress toward your goal and revise it as necessary. Setting a timetable helps you determine when you have achieved your action steps toward meeting your final goal.

x

SECTION II - PROACTIVE LISTENING STRATEGIES

SECTION II - Proactive Listening Strategies
In this section, you'll learn about the primary elements conducive to proactive listening and the questioning techniques you can employ to enhance this style. You'll learn about:
- becoming an active listener,
- becoming an effective listener,
- • using questioning methods.

PROACTIVE LISTENING STRATEGIES

Proactive listening strategies

Do you know someone who has an ability for really listening to others in almost any situation at work?

If you know someone with that ability, do you want to develop the same listening skill yourself? You can, you know. You can become a proactive listener by following several simple, straightforward methods.

Proactive listening is nothing more complex than using learned listening methods to avoid difficulties when you're communicating with others--in this case, your co-workers or employees.

Question

Given your job responsibilities, you don't have time to waste. So when you meet with an employee or co-worker, you want to make the time count and be productive. A good way to make the best use of your time is to be a proactive listener.

Do you believe you're ready to be a proactive listener?

Options

1. not ready at all

2. unready
3. not sure
4. ready
5. very ready

Answer

If you rated yourself less than ready, examine both the benefits of proactive listening and the methods essential for developing your listening skills.

You can gain other people's respect when you're a proactive listener. Why? Because they can see that you actually want to hear what they have to tell you.

Excellent communication skills require the ability to listen to--and hear--others. When you use proactive listening strategies, you can develop better rapport with others, gain insight into their concerns, and be seen as a morale booster because you've paid attention to them. If you're a manager or supervisor, when your staff members realize you actually are listening to them, you may see their morale improve. Proactive listening fosters a valuable win-win situation for everyone.

Question

You're going to communicate with others throughout your professional life. It's your choice whether you communicate poorly or well. Select the statements that show the value of using proactive listening strategies when communicating with other people in the workplace.

Options

1. Listening strategies offer guidelines to follow with problem people.

2. Listening strategies give you insight into others' concerns.

3. Listening strategies can help you develop rapport with others.

4. Listening strategies enable you to avoid conflict with other personnel.

5. Listening strategies can lead to improved morale among workers.

Answer

Actually, listening strategies help you develop rapport and understand staff concerns as well as improve employee morale.

Option 1: Incorrect. Listening strategies are nothing more than methods to avoid difficulties when you're communicating with others. The value of proactive listening strategies is that they help you in any situation, with any type of person.

Option 2: Correct. When you listen, you actually hear what your employees are saying. A benefit of using proactive listening strategies is that when people realize you paid attention to them, they are more open to sharing their concerns.

Option 3: Correct. A benefit of using proactive listening strategies is that when people know you are interested in them, you develop rapport with them. Listening strategies let people see that you actually want to hear what they have to tell you.

Option 4: Incorrect. Listening strategies aren't a way of avoiding conflict but a way of avoiding difficulties in communicating. Proactive listening strategies don't help you avoid talking altogether, but do aid in better communication with others.

Option 5: This choice is correct. Proactive listening strategies are a way of paying attention to people and

Assertive Communication

their input. When employees feel they are heard and appreciated, their morale is improved.

ASSESSING AN INTERACTION IN A BUSINESS SCENARIO

Assessing an interaction in a business scenario
"It takes two to speak the truth--one to speak and one to hear." --Henry David Thoreau, American naturalist and writer
Question
An assertive professional interacts with others by listening and hearing what they have to say. Listening and hearing are essential components of a proactive listening strategy.

Do you believe you hear the message other people in the workplace are trying to tell you?
Options
1. don't hear at all
2. don't hear well
3. undecided
4. hear well
5. hear very well
Answer

Assertive Communication

Regardless of how well you hear the message, you need to pay close attention to the primary elements of being an effective listener.

It's important to be an effective listener as well as an active listener. The two listening styles complement each other and make you a good communicator, which in turn contributes to your abilities to be an efficient business professional. In this topic, you'll learn about three primary elements of being an effective listener and see examples. You'll also learn how to discern the elements in real-life situations in business settings.

The three necessary elements of effective listening are:
- concentrating on the message,
- summarizing the discussion,
- providing a reasonable response.

The value of being an active listener includes projecting a positive image to others and keeping an open mind when you talk to them. There's an equally important effective listening strategy to follow in order to become a proactive listener and an assertive business professional. The first element of an effective listening strategy is to concentrate on the message to "hear" the content of what someone is telling you. This element contains three components.

Open the conversation

You want to open the conversation and put everyone at ease in an atmosphere that fosters good communication. When opening a conversation, it's essential to clarify the reason the conversation is taking place and to make sure everyone has the same agenda and expectations.

Focus on the ideas

You want to listen to hear the message. To do so, you need to focus on the ideas or issues being presented. What is the core idea? Are you dealing with facts, opinions, or both? Most important, do you think you understand the ideas or issues the other person is trying to convey?

Analyze nonverbal cues

It's important to pay attention to the nonverbal image the other person presents. What do tone of voice and body language convey to you? Is the person at ease, nervous, or upset? Notice these cues as you listen, and then work to foster a productive conversation.

Question

Based on what you've just learned, which statements illustrate focusing on the other person's message?

Options

1. Pay attention to nonverbal indicators.
2. Close the discussion decisively.
3. Concentrate on the person's core ideas.
4. Open the discussion effectively.
5. Make the person feel welcome.

Answer

Actually, in order to concentrate on the message, you need to open the discussion and then focus on the ideas presented to you. You also need to pay attention to nonverbal cues during the discussion.

Option 1: This option is correct. Analyzing non-verbal cues is a way of concentrating on the message, which is one of the elements of effective listening.

Option 2: This option is incorrect. Closing the discussion does not illustrate focusing on the other person's message. Rather, opening a discussion effectively is a way of focusing on what the other person is saying.

Assertive Communication

Option 3: This is a correct option. Concentrating on the main ideas is a way of concentrating on the person's message, which is one of the elements of effective listening. Focusing on their ideas allows you to hear what they are saying.

Option 4: Correct. This statement illustrates focusing on others' messages. When you focus on listening to another person, you will open the conversation to invite him to speak his mind.

$t.getLocalizedString("transcript.option") 5: This is an incorrect option. While making a person feel welcome is valuable in being an active listener, it is not a strategy for focusing on what a person is saying.

The second effective listening element requires you to summarize your conversation. This is a good idea in many circumstances, but it's imperative in a business situation. Summarizing keeps you on track and helps ensure that miscommunication doesn't occur.

Employee 1

"I've had trouble with the procedure and I'm not the only one. It's too complicated and poorly presented. It reads like a regulation from the federal government."

Employee 2

"I don't hear you saying, 'Throw out the procedure.' What I think you're saying is that we need to rewrite it to be understandable and present it in an organized fashion."

The woman on the previous page summarized her co-worker's comments as expressing the need for rewriting the procedure rather than throwing it out. She also interpreted his comments as requiring a different, understandable presentation of the procedure following its rewrite.

The third element that makes up an effective listening strategy involves providing a reasonable response to comments made by the other person during a conversation.

Brad: I think I understand the reason you wanted to meet. You're concerned about the draft of the quality assurance procedure, aren't you?

Kate: That's right. I hope I'm not being too pushy, but I do have some concerns I'd like to discuss, if that's OK.

Brad: Sure. That's fine. I appreciate the fact that you're voicing your concerns to me. What is it specifically that bothers you about the procedure?

Kate: Actually, I think the procedure itself is fine. I'm bothered by the lack of specificity about its review and renewal.

Brad: OK. You think the procedure is acceptable as written. But you recommend that we strengthen the section that specifies the procedure's review and renewal cycle. Is that correct?

Kate: Yes, it is. I think the "review as necessary" clause should be replaced with a specific time frame.

Brad: I agree. That's a good suggestion. I'll bring it up when the drafting committee meets next week to review the procedure. And Kate, thanks for being open in presenting your concerns. I appreciate that.

Brad did an excellent job of providing a reasonable response to Kate by acknowledging her concerns and noting the action step he would take as a result of their conversation.

Question

Before you can be an effective listener, you need to have a thorough understanding of the three elements of

Assertive Communication

that listening strategy. Select the primary elements of effective listening.

Options

1. Make a reasonable effort to summarize the conversation.
2. Display a positive image to others during a conversation.
3. Ensure that you provide a reasonable response.
4. Try to make the conversation profitable.
5. Ensure that you concentrate on the message being delivered.

Answers

Actually, in an effective listening strategy, the listener concentrates on the message in order to summarize and to respond in a reasonable manner.

Option 1: This is a correct option. Summarizing your conversation is the second element of effective listening. Summarizing a conversation keeps you on track and helps ensure that miscommunication doesn't occur.

Option 2: This is not a correct option. Displaying a positive image is valuable for being an active listener but it is not one of the three elements of effective listening.

Option 3: Correct. Providing a reasonable response is the third element of effective listening. By providing a reasonable response, you acknowledge what the other person has said. This demonstrates that you have listened to the other person.

Option 4: Incorrect. Trying to make the conversation profitable is a goal, not an element of effective listening. The goal of effective listening is to avoid difficulties in communication or miscommunications.

Option 5: This option is correct. Concentrating on the message is the first element of listening and helps you hear what the other person is saying.

These questions will help you identify if you're actually practicing the elements of effective listening.

- Did I focus on the message being delivered?
- Did I summarize the conversation?
- Did I provide a reasonable response?

Ed and June are on the company's charitable giving committee. Ed has just made a rambling statement about the need for criteria. June responds by restating what she thinks Ed's key points are: criteria for organizations to be on the charitable list and criteria to set the amount available to any one group. June mentions that the discussion indicates all committee members are in agreement with Ed and then suggests that criteria be at the top of the agenda for the committee's next meeting.

USING ASSERTIVE QUESTIONING

Using assertive questioning

Most business professionals have experienced situations in which it was essential to ask the right questions to maintain a productive conversation. Do you make a point of asking the right questions?

Question

Asking effective questions is something you can learn to do. Which methods do you believe illustrate a questioning style that supports being an assertive business professional?

Options

1. asking clarifying questions
2. asking feeling questions
3. asking nonsensitive questions
4. asking for constructive suggestions
5. asking noncontroversial questions

Answers

Actually, effective questions include clarifying questions, feeling questions, and questions eliciting constructive suggestions.

Option 1: This option is correct. The method of clarifying questions will help you focus on and clarify core ideas or issues in a discussion. They also will help you ensure that you don't misunderstand what someone is saying.

Option 2: This option is correct. Asking feeling questions is an effective method because it allows you to address sensitive issues and gain useful insights into your peers' or subordinates' thinking.

Option 3: Incorrect. You should not ask nonsensitive questions because they are not effective. Rather you want to ask feeling questions that are sensitive to people's concerns or needs because they allow you to address sensitive issues.

Option 4: This option is correct. The method of asking for constructive ideas almost guarantees receipt of useful suggestions and ideas as you get others engaged in helpful discussions.

Option 5: This option is incorrect. Noncontroversial questions may be ineffective in matters where sensitive feelings are involved and thus would not elicit helpful information or may fail to elicit constructive suggestions to a hard topic.

In this topic, you'll learn how to use questioning methods to elicit constructive answers from those with whom you engage in conversation in the workplace. Three primary questioning methods are:
- asking clarifying questions,
- asking feeling questions,
- asking for constructive suggestions.

An assertive professional can use effective questioning methods in a variety of business settings. To note just two common examples, you can definitely use questioning methods as you help a co-worker discuss a problem or as you give constructive criticism to an employee.

The first method is to ask clarifying questions. Clarifying questions help focus on and clarify core ideas or issues in a discussion. They also help ensure that you don't misunderstand what someone is saying.

Jill is having a long conversation with Rebecca, another employee in the training department where they both work. Rebecca recently had a difficult time on a training assignment at their company's regional headquarters in New England. Rebecca thought that both staff and trainees reacted poorly to her presence. Jill has employed an assertive questioning style to encourage Rebecca to talk about the problem assignment.

The issue

What do you think was the main issue? Or what was the single most important reason you had difficulties on this assignment? If you can identify the core of the problem, it will allow you to take steps to avoid a similar problem on your next assignment.

The approach

Do you think the staff and trainees received adequate notice to schedule the training? Did trainees get a briefing that explained why they were receiving the training and, more important, how the training would help them on the job?

The solution

What can you do proactively to make things better for you on your next regional training assignment? How can you work with regional staff to ensure a better training outcome for you, for them, and for the trainees?

Jill did an excellent job of asking clarifying questions intended to help Rebecca identify what went wrong. Asking if the staff and trainees had received notice of the training directly addressed Rebecca's feeling that her presence was not welcomed at the regional headquarters.

And, more important, Jill asked Rebecca what she could do in the future to ensure success on a training project. Jill's troubleshooting questions were intended to help Rebecca solve problems.

The second questioning method is to ask feeling questions; for example, "How do you feel about this feedback?" This method allows you to address sensitive issues and gain useful insights into your peers' or subordinates' thinking.

Asking feeling questions can be a productive, though difficult, method to use. They're difficult because many people have trouble dealing with feelings, especially in the workplace. However, once you become comfortable with this questioning method, you may find it very helpful.

Gather information

"I have trouble confronting feelings, mine or others'. My mentor helped me become comfortable asking this type of question and I now use it frequently to gather information."

Gain insights

"I gain useful insights asking how people feel about issues or concerns. Learning to ask feeling questions enhanced my ability to listen to others at work."

Feeling questions can range across a spectrum from personal to strictly work-related. On one level, you may find yourself asking a co-worker how he feels about an upcoming performance review or how he feels about his modified job assignment. At another level, you may ask a work-focused question such as how someone feels about the new procedures just put in place by upper management.

Once you overcome any difficulties you may encounter when you begin using this questioning method, you may find that it enhances your ability to truly listen to and hear what co-workers and peers have to say on sensitive subjects.

You can obtain lots of ideas when you use the third questioning method, which involves asking for constructive ideas. This questioning method almost guarantees receipt of useful suggestions and constructive ideas as you get others engaged in helpful discussions.

Brainstorming

Ask co-workers for suggestions all the time. Invite them to brainstorming sessions. It's amazing how many good ideas are generated this way.

Ideas for growth

Ask employees for their ideas on what would help them grow and improve. When they're engaged, you'll develop lots of useful ideas together that benefit both of you.

Make it a point to ask numerous sources for constructive suggestions whenever it would be helpful to you. The ideas they generate can help you be a successful business professional.

Patricia, a sales representative for a large software company, is meeting with Jim, another salesperson. In this case, Patricia is helping Jim evaluate a difficult sales call he recently made to a large West Coast client.

Clarifying questions

"Let's focus on the actual call. Can you identify one or two specific reasons you found this sales call to be especially difficult? Was it your preparation? The person you called on? Or some other factor you can identify?"

Feeling questions

"How do you feel about the way the sales call went with the client? More important, how do you feel about the way you personally handled the call and the interaction with the buyer you were meeting with?"

Constructive ideas

"What ideas or suggestions do you have for changing how you'll conduct your next sales call on this client? Have you thought about asking a few of us to brainstorm ideas with you? I'd be glad to do that. I'd probably get some good ideas myself."

Patricia did a good job of applying her knowledge of the three separate questioning methods to help Jim discuss a difficult sales call experience.

To use questioning methods effectively, there are a few points to remember. Asking clarifying questions will help you focus on and clarify core issues and also avoid misunderstandings. When you ask feeling questions, you gain useful insights as you address sensitive issues. Finally, remember that when you ask for constructive suggestions, you can gain useful ideas as well as engage others in discussion that can be of value to all involved.

SECTION III - CONSTRUCTIVE FEEDBACK STRATEGY

SECTION III - Constructive Feedback Strategy

In this section, you'll learn about a constructive feedback strategy as well as steps to follow and methods to employ to provide constructive feedback to others in the work force. You'll learn about:
- clarifying your feedback strategy,
- giving positive feedback,
- providing constructive criticism,
- saying no responsibly.

USING CONSTRUCTIVE FEEDBACK STRATEGIES

Using constructive feedback strategies

Do you frequently dread those times when you're required to provide feedback to someone? Why not try using a constructive feedback strategy?

Question

Jacquelyn, a co-worker in the accounting division, just let you in on her secret. She always uses a constructive strategy when providing feedback to others. She suggested that you try the same approach. Do you believe the following statement is true or false?

The ability to use a constructive feedback strategy isn't a gift, it's an approach that can be learned by any competent business professional.

Options

1. true
2. false

Answer

Actually, some people instinctively seem to know the right thing to say. But most people with the ability to provide constructive feedback weren't born with the gift; they worked hard to learn the necessary skills.

Option 1: This statement is true. Providing constructive feedback is saying the right things, in the right way, at the right time, to the right person. It does not require a special gift or talent.

Option 2: This statement is not false. Any competent business professional can learn effective methods for providing constructive feedback. This strategy does not require a special gift or talent.

A constructive feedback strategy includes saying the right things, in the right way, at the right time, to the right person. Sounds relatively simple, doesn't it? In actual practice, it's not always that easy. But when you know effective methods for providing constructive feedback, things start to fall into place. And you can stop dreading the feedback session, whether it's with a co-worker, employee, or even your supervisor.

The professional benefits of using a constructive feedback strategy are:
- establishing accountability,
- improving productivity,
- lessening workplace stress.

Question

Based on what you've just learned, what are benefits of using a constructive feedback strategy as part of your professional repertoire?

Options

1. You can enhance your image as a professional.
2. You can help reduce stress in the workplace for others.

3. You can halt negative interactions between employees.

4. You can foster an increase in everyone's productivity.

5. You can help establish accountability for employees.

Answer

Actually, three of the items above indicate benefits of using a constructive feedback strategy--establishing accountability, increasing productivity, and reducing stress in the workplace.

Option 1: This option is incorrect. Enhancing your image as a professional is not a benefit of using a constructive feedback strategy. Benefits of constructive feedback focus on benefits to the entire work environment, not just to yourself.

Option 2: This option is correct. A benefit of constructive feedback includes reducing stress in the workplace for others. It makes feedback sessions less stressful when people know to anticipate helpful input.

Option 3: This option is incorrect. Constructive feedback will not stop negative interactions altogether, although the benefits of lowering stress, increasing productivity and establishing accountability may lead to fewer negative interactions.

Option 4: This option is correct. Another benefit to using a constructive feedback strategy is that it improves productivity by providing people information they can use to improve their work habits.

$t.getLocalizedString("transcript.option") 5: This option is correct. Using a constructive feedback strategy establishes accountability because it clearly outlines expectations and means of improvement.

STEPS TO CLARIFY THE FEEDBACK STRATEGY

Steps to clarify the feedback strategy

How often have you heard something to the effect of "Feedback? I'm uneasy giving it, and recipients can be resistant. They often don't want to receive feedback"?

Clarifying your strategy now can help you feel prepared and confident as you give constructive feedback in the future. In this topic, you'll learn about three steps to help you clarify the constructive feedback strategy. You'll learn about:

- adopting an effective personal feedback style,
- meeting feedback criteria,
- using appropriate timing.

The first step is to adopt an effective personal feedback style. Your style is the way you conduct yourself as you provide feedback to others. Once you've adopted an effective style, you're a step closer to giving constructive feedback in the workplace.

being courteous

The assertive professional style and the constructive feedback strategy both rely heavily on courteous behavior. Your courtesy will put others at ease and foster their hearing the feedback you're providing. Courtesy is essential to the constructive feedback strategy.

being truthful

It's essential to be truthful in the feedback you give others. In fact, feedback's useless unless it is truthful. Your task is to provide the truth in a way that's sensitive to others' feelings while also getting the feedback message across to them.

being positive

Being positive is a useful component of this strategy. Your positive attitude can help others receive and act on the feedback you give them. Remember that your task is to be positive even when the feedback contains criticism.

Question

Match each aspect of an effective personal feedback style with the statement that best describes it.

Options

A. being courteous
B. being truthful
C. being positive

Targets

1. "There's a problem with your report. Let's discuss it."
2. "I'm glad you came in. I'd like us to have an open discussion."
3. "We've identified an issue; now let's see how to resolve it."

Answers

Actually, the correct answers are indicated above. It's important to understand the courteous, truthful, and positive aspects of an effective personal feedback style.

By stating that a problem exists in an employee's work, you are being truthful and providing feedback that will help him improve. Not being truthful about the problem does not allow the employee to learn or grow.

Courtesy is essential to the constructive feedback strategy. In being courteous about feedback, you create an open environment where the employee can speak and you can listen.

By being positive, you focus on the resolution of a problem instead of dwelling on it, or blaming. You develop solutions an employee can use for improvement.

You will feel more self-assured using the constructive feedback strategy after you've adopted an effective personal feedback style and grown accustomed to its use.

The second step is to meet the necessary feedback criteria.

Objective

"Objectivity is essential. To me, that means dealing with observable facts and avoiding the distortion caused when personal feelings or prejudices are present. At times, I find this ideal difficult to achieve, but it's a good goal to try to reach on a consistent basis."

Specific

"Being specific is important when you're providing feedback. Recipients of vague, general statements just aren't helped by such remarks. So I'm specific; I reference known events, specific times, objective observations, and predictable outcomes."

Descriptive

"I always strive to be descriptive. For me, that requires providing a context for presenting facts and observations. This approach allows me to put some life into a conversation that, otherwise, could be a sterile presentation."

Meeting these feedback criteria can help you remain focused on providing feedback that is useful and constructive.

Question

Based on what you've just learned, select the statements that illustrate effective feedback criteria.

Options

1. It's useful to state specific facts, times, and events.
2. It's helpful to be descriptive in your statements.
3. It's helpful to make subjective statements.
4. It's important to make objective statements.
5. It's important to make inclusive statements.

Answer

Actually, the feedback criteria are being objective, specific, and descriptive.

Option 1: This option is correct. Stating specifics is helpful when providing feedback because it provides facts that can be addressed or measured. Vague feedback or references do not provide enough information.

Option 2: Correct. It is helpful to be descriptive in your statements because this provides a context for presenting facts and observations. In addition, being descriptive can put life into a presentation or discussion that would otherwise be sterile.

Option 3: Incorrect. Making objective statements is more effective than subjective statements because you deal

Assertive Communication

with observable facts and avoid the distortion caused when personal feelings or prejudices are present.

Option 4: This option is correct. In developing a constructive feedback strategy it is important to make objective statements because they help avoid the distortion caused when personal feelings or prejudices are present.

Option 5: This is an incorrect choice. Inclusive statements are not effective feedback because they do not provide enough information or details for the recipient to act upon.

The third step is to use appropriate timing. That is, when is it the right time to give constructive feedback to someone in the workplace?

Follow along as Michele provides constructive feedback to Brent, one of her staff members.

Michele: Brent, I'd like to talk to you about your current project. There's some feedback I'd like to give you before you move on to the next phase.

Brent: Is there a problem? I thought the project was moving along fairly well--no major problems or client issues.

Michele: You're right. It's nothing major, but I do have some ideas I want to discuss with you and this seems like a good time.

Brent: I guess so. It would be helpful to get your feedback before moving into Phase 2--especially if there's a problem I can resolve.

Michele: I think a conversation would be helpful. I have time either Wednesday afternoon or Thursday morning. Which would work best for you?

Brent: Well, does anyone else need to be there? If it's just the two of us, then I'd prefer Wednesday afternoon. That would give me more time to deal with the outcome of our discussion--especially if it changes the project timeline or plan.

Michele: Wednesday afternoon would be fine. Let's schedule for 2 p.m. in my office. It'll be just the two of us. And my feedback won't affect the plan or schedule, although it could influence the product in some ways.

Brent: OK. Wednesday it is. I'll look forward to getting your ideas. I want the product to really please our client, and I'll take positive ideas at any time.

Michele determined the appropriate timing to talk to Brent. She arranged to provide feedback after Phase 1 of the project--feedback that could be helpful during Phase 2. She also set a day and time that worked for both her and Brent's schedules.

Appropriate timing for providing constructive feedback can be as basic as determining the most convenient time of day or day of the week. Timing can also be important because of the way it affects project schedules or plans.

Question

Before you can be successful at clarifying the constructive feedback strategy, you need to have a thorough understanding of the strategy's three steps. Select the primary steps involved in clarifying a constructive feedback strategy.

Options

1. Avoid sensitive topics when providing feedback.
2. Adopt an effective personal feedback style.
3. Use appropriate timing for giving feedback.
4. Acknowledge someone's need for feedback.

5. Meet criteria for providing feedback.

Answers

The three steps are adopting an effective style, meeting criteria, and using appropriate timing.

Option 1: Incorrect. Avoiding sensitive or difficult topics is not one of the primary steps involved in clarifying a constructive feedback strategy. In fact, constructive feedback strategies help address sensitive topics to achieve a positive outcome.

Option 2: Correct. Adopting a personal feedback style will help you clarify a constructive feedback strategy because you'll feel better about giving feedback and focus on being courteous, truthful and positive.

Option 3: Correct. Using appropriate timing helps you to clarify a constructive feedback strategy and is important both for having conversations at convenient times and for making sure project schedules and plans move along as they should.

Option 4: This option is incorrect. Acknowledging a need for feedback is not one of the steps for clarifying a constructive feedback strategy. However, it is a precursor to providing constructive feedback.

Option 5: This option is correct. Meeting the three criteria for providing feedback--objectivity, specifics, and descriptive information--will ensure that you provide effective feedback.

There are specific questions to ask to assess whether or not you're actually following the steps to successfully clarify the constructive feedback strategy.

Adopt an effective personal feedback style

Have you adopted an effective personal feedback style?

Meet the necessary feedback criteria

Have you met feedback criteria?

Use appropriate timing

How was your timing in providing feedback? Will your timing help ensure that feedback is heard by and helpful to the recipient?

Kim has decided to be helpful by giving Peggy, a co-worker, feedback about an inappropriate workplace behavior as well as a suggestion for avoiding it in the future. Kim has two specific instances she can tell Peggy about in which Kim was an uninvolved observer. Kim's decided to ask Peggy out to lunch at a time that's mutually convenient so they can talk in a friendly, private environment. Kim wants to make her suggestions before Peggy exhibits the behavior again.

Kim did a good job of planning to provide constructive feedback to Peggy. Kim used the three steps to clarify her feedback strategy.

Adopt an effective personal feedback style

Kim planned to truthfully say what she saw as Peggy's inappropriate behavior. She was also prepared to be courteous and provide a positive idea to Peggy for avoiding the behavior in the future. Kim has adopted an effective personal style.

Meet the necessary feedback criteria

Kim was clear about following feedback criteria. She was an objective observer of specific examples of Peggy's behavior. Kim was prepared to give descriptive feedback to Peggy. Kim met the criteria necessary to achieve her goal of giving Peggy constructive feedback.

Use appropriate timing

Kim was aware of the need to use appropriate timing to provide feedback to Peggy. In this instance, she chose the lunch hour, when they both had time available. She also hoped to talk to Peggy soon, before the behavior occurred again.

Kim's careful adherence to style, criteria, and timing should ensure a successful feedback session with her friend Peggy. You can also be successful at clarifying a constructive feedback strategy if you follow these three steps.

In this topic, you learned that those steps are:
- adopting an effective personal feedback style,
- meeting feedback criteria,
- using appropriate timing.

STEPS NECESSARY TO GIVE POSITIVE FEEDBACK

Steps necessary to give positive feedback

Most business professionals have provided feedback to someone. Of course, if you're a supervisor, you've probably given feedback on numerous occasions. And, like other assertive business professionals, you'd like all feedback sessions to be productive and well-received.

The good news is that there are useful steps you can take to increase the likelihood of achieving a positive outcome from the feedback sessions you conduct with others in the workplace. The steps are logical, and they're remarkably easy to learn. In this topic, you'll learn about three steps for providing positive feedback to others:
- reviewing goals,
- describing performance,
- reinforcing positive behavior.

The first step toward ensuring a positive outcome from a feedback session is to review goals. This can encompass someone's personal goals in the workplace as well as goals resulting from a job assignment.

Assertive Communication

Reviewing goals is necessary when you're requested, or required, to provide feedback to someone in the workplace. A goals review provides a focus and enables you to set the stage for describing a person's performance in pursuit of that goal.

Goals

"At the start of a feedback session, I check to ensure that both he and I clearly understand his goal that I'm discussing in my feedback."

Agreement

"I want to reach mutual agreement because the goals are the basis for providing feedback on his actual performance in the workplace."

Beginning a feedback session with a review of goals lets you start in a positive way because goals are concrete and are accepted as a basis for performance assessments and feedback in the workplace.

The second step toward ensuring a positive outcome from a feedback session is to describe a person's actual performance. You should do so in a way that's objective and descriptive.

Follow along as Denise, a publishing supervisor, provides feedback to Jerome during a one-on-one performance review.

Denise: Jerome, now that we've had the opportunity to review your performance goals for this year, do you have any questions?

Jerome: No, I don't. We agreed on the goals at the start of the year, and I make a point of checking my progress each month to make sure I'm on track.

Denise: That's a good idea. I wish everyone were as thorough. In fact, I've observed that you're good about meeting milestones and final deadlines. That certainly helps others in the process to meet their deadlines too.

Jerome: Thanks. I try to hand materials off on time so the editors and artists can stay on the timeline to meet their deadlines. I realize how important it is for the products to get to the client when promised.

Denise: I've also noticed the excellent quality of your work. I've seen definite improvement this year in what you're producing. Just keep up the good work.

Jerome: OK. I appreciate the mentoring you've provided. And I also worked hard to learn from past mistakes. I guess that's all paid off.

Denise: Yes, I think it has. Your efforts have enabled you to meet deadlines with quality products, and that meets your major annual goal. Now let's talk about your secondary goal.

Jerome: Sure. But first let me just say that I appreciate your feedback.

Denise did an excellent job of presenting Jerome's performance in terms of observable actions. And she was objective and descriptive. This approach enabled Denise to maintain a positive tone throughout the performance review.

The third step toward ensuring a positive outcome from a feedback session is to reinforce positive behavior.

Your feedback should be designed to help others recognize what they're doing well and how their actions or behaviors help the organization. Feedback then should encourage them to continue their positive behavior.

Recognize good behavior

When you tell others they're doing well, be sure to identify those specific actions and behaviors that you think

Assertive Communication

contribute to their success. When they recognize what's beneficial, they're much more likely to continue to exhibit those actions and behaviors in the workplace.

Describe its impact

The positive feedback you provide others can be enhanced by stating specifically how their actions or behaviors help the organization achieve its goals. This is an excellent way to put their positive actions and behaviors in an actual context in the workplace.

Question

Before you can be effective at providing positive feedback, you need to have a thorough understanding of the three steps of that strategy. What are the steps?

Options

1. Make sure to describe a person's actual performance.

2. Ensure that you review goals at the start of a feedback session.

3. Make sure to avoid a description of negative behavior.

4. Take action to reinforce a person's positive behaviors.

5. Ensure that not too much emphasis is placed on positive behaviors.

Answers

Actually, in a positive feedback strategy you review goals and then describe actual performance. Finally, you reinforce positive behaviors.

Option 1: Correct. Describing performance is the second step toward providing positive feedback, by doing so you stay objective and base the discussion on observable behavior. You also provide detailed descriptions that are helpful.

Option 2: This is a correct option. Reviewing goals is the first step toward providing positive feedback. A goals review provides a focus and enables you to set the stage for describing a person's performance in pursuit of that goal.

Option 3: This option is incorrect. This is not one of the steps toward providing positive feedback. Rather, one of the steps is describing the person's actual performance, which may include describing negative behavior.

Option 4: Correct. Reinforcing positive behaviors is the third step toward providing positive feedback. By recognizing people's positive behaviors, you help others recognize what they are doing well and how their actions or behaviors help the organization.

Option 5: This option is incorrect. Actually, emphasizing positive behaviors is one of the three strategies. By emphasizing positive behavior, you note what employees are doing well so it will be continued or repeated.

Now that you've practiced identifying the three steps involved in giving positive feedback, you're ready to assess whether you're actually following these steps.

Review goals

The first question to ask is: Did I review goals at the beginning of the feedback session? Remember that goals can pertain to someone's personal goals in the workplace as well as goals resulting from a job assignment.

Describe performance

Next, ask yourself: Did I describe actual performance during the feedback session? Your comments should be as objective and specific as you can make them.

Reinforce positive behavior

Assertive Communication

Finally, ask: Did I reinforce positive behaviors during the feedback session? You can deliver reinforcing statements during the session and also to end it on a positive note.

Alberto and Fred both work in a bank's loan department. Fred has asked Alberto to help him prepare for his six- month review. Alberto accepted and asked Fred to list things he's done on the job and to note areas where he wants to improve. He also asked Fred to note where his actions pertain to the six-month goals he was given. In their talk, Alberto tells Fred what he's observed Fred doing well and how that contributes to the bank's success and encourages Fred to continue those behaviors.

Were you able to identify the details that make this an example of Alberto's success at giving positive feedback?

Review goals

In assessing the situation, it's clear that Alberto knows it's important to tie Fred's actions and behaviors to his six-month goals.

Describe performance

Alberto asked Fred to describe his own performance. Alberto also added comments about his own observations of Fred's performance at the bank.

Reinforce positive behavior

Finally, it's clear that Alberto was reinforcing Fred's positive behaviors. Alberto was providing encouragement and telling Fred specifically what, in Alberto's opinion, Fred was doing that would lead to success at the bank.

Giving positive feedback contributes to the self-assurance and eventual success of people in the workplace. When you give positive feedback as an assertive business professional, you help build a positive work environment.

You can use a positive feedback strategy to good effect in the workplace. You can foster others' professional growth when you help them review their goals and performance and when your support reinforces their positive behavior.

METHODS FOR GIVING CONSTRUCTIVE CRITICISM

Methods for giving constructive criticism

"The trouble with most of us is that we would rather be ruined by praise than saved by criticism." --Norman Vincent Peale, American clergyman and author

In this topic, you'll learn how to provide constructive criticism to others in the workplace. Three primary methods that you'll learn to use are:
- focusing on the current issue,
- focusing on observable actions or behaviors,
- focusing on a plan of action.

Question

Constructive criticism involves identifying a specific current issue and giving critical feedback that contains suggestions for altering the actions or behaviors that led to the criticism being given.

How comfortable are you in providing constructive criticism to others?

Options

1. not comfortable

2. somewhat uncomfortable
3. neutral
4. comfortable
5. very comfortable

Answer

Regardless of your comfort level, there are methods you can use to improve your ability to give constructive criticism.

The first method is to focus on a current issue. You can achieve the best results when you also limit your constructive criticism to a single issue. Don't bring past issues into the current discussion unless it's essential to do so. For example, in an ongoing corrective action for a problem employee, you may need to reference previous action steps and decisions. In general, however, you don't want multiple--or past--issues to distract from the constructive criticism you're providing in the current feedback session.

You can be very specific when you focus on one current issue. Specificity is essential to constructive criticism in identifying both the issue and its impact on others or the organization as a whole.

Andrea, a senior employee in a large architectural firm, is talking to a junior draftsman, Jordan. Andrea is Jordan's mentor, and she's holding her weekly scheduled meeting with Jordan to give him feedback on his work. She's given positive feedback and is now providing Jordan with some constructive criticism.

The issue

"Jordan, there's an issue with last Friday's deadline. You accepted the deadline during the weekly planning session and then failed to meet it. That's a problem."

Assertive Communication

Its impact

"It's an issue because missing deadlines delays the schedule for getting drawings to our client. And the project's success depends on meeting client expectations."

Andrea's constructive criticism identified one specific issue: Jordan's failure to meet a deadline. She then identified the effect on the company: The entire schedule slipped, and the client's expectations may not be met.

The second method is to focus on observable actions or behaviors. This approach encourages you to be objective, as well as specific, in providing constructive criticism.

Actions

"I noticed that you weren't following the prescribed procedures for producing the monthly sales reports. Do I need to explain their importance?"

Behaviors

"You acted very annoyed in this morning's team meeting, yet you said nothing. I'd like you to speak up if something bothers you rather than behaving negatively."

In one instance, the previous constructive criticism identified a specific action: not following procedures. In the other instance, the criticism identified an undesirable negative behavior.

The third method is to determine a plan of action to address the issue or behavior that is the subject of the constructive criticism. The plan, which you should help the person develop, should identify specific actions for her to take or behaviors for her to change. It's most effective if you set specific times for her to accomplish given milestones and times to get together to review her progress. These steps help ensure that your criticism really is constructive.

Follow along as Anna, a human resources specialist, helps Vincent, a bookkeeping supervisor, develop an action plan in response to her suggestions.

Anna: Vincent, are we in agreement that we're addressing the issue of your completing quarterly personnel reviews by the deadlines called for in the procedures?

Vincent: Yes. That's the issue. Now that we've talked, I realize the importance of getting the reviews done on time and submitting the paperwork. I didn't realize I was holding up other processes.

Anna: Good. I thought it might just be a misunderstanding, and I'm glad you realize the importance of the procedure. I think it would be helpful for you to develop a calendar with the dates for scheduling and conducting your reviews.

Vincent: That's a good idea. My schedule should probably also include the dates the reviews are due to you.

Anna: Do you think you can have the calendar developed by the end of the month? I'd like to meet with you to review it.

Vincent: Sure, that's no problem. That will ensure I get it done sooner rather than later.

Anna: Once the calendar is finalized, we can touch base at each milestone to make sure you're on schedule. How does that sound?

Vincent: That sounds fine. I can use this process elsewhere as well. Thanks for the suggestion.

Anna ensured that she and Vincent were focused on the same issue. She then helped Vincent identify specific actions he could take to address the issue.

Assertive Communication

Question

Before you can effectively provide constructive criticism, you need to have a thorough understanding of the three methods of that element of the constructive feedback strategy. What are these methods?

Options

1. Ensure that you develop a viable plan of action.
2. Ensure that the feedback avoids involving specific people.
3. Make sure to focus on a single, current issue.
4. Make sure to present observed actions or behaviors.
5. Make sure to avoid issues that could be too sensitive.

Answers

Actually, in constructive criticism you focus on a single issue and discuss observed actions or behaviors. Then you address that issue in a plan of action.

Option 1: This option is correct. Focusing on a plan of action is one of the three methods of effectively providing constructive criticism. A plan of action will identify specific actions for an employee to take or behaviors to change.

Option 2: This is an incorrect option. Constructive feedback must be specific at every level. Specificity is essential to constructive criticism in identifying both the issue and its impact on others or the organization as a whole.

Option 3: Correct. One method of effectively providing constructive criticism is focusing on the current issue. Bringing in past or other incidents clouds the issue and makes it more complex.

Option 4: This option is correct. By detailing observed actions and behaviors, you are presenting the criticism objectively as well as providing specifics. This is an effective method of providing constructive criticism.

Option 5: This option is incorrect. The goal of constructive feedback is improvement, not avoidance. Regardless of your comfort level with a topic, providing constructive criticism is a way of being an assertive professional.

Now that you've practiced identifying the three methods involved in providing constructive criticism, you're ready to assess whether you're actually following these methods.

Did I focus the criticism on a single, current issue?

Remember that it's distracting to deal with more than one issue or to let past issues get entangled in your current discussion and criticism.

Did I focus on observed actions or behaviors?

This focus helps avoid the possibility of personality differences becoming involved in your criticism and allows you to be objective in your presentation of the issue.

Did I help determine a plan of action?

The plan should address positive actions or a change in behaviors. It should also identify milestones and ongoing ways to communicate about the success of the plan as it is put into action.

Della and Izzat are co-workers in a fast-food chain's national headquarters. Izzat has just mentioned Della's failure to get reports done on time, particularly the regions' last quarterly production reports. Izzat says she hasn't observed Della putting much time into gathering the data needed for the reports. Della responds defensively. She's reluctant to talk about Izzat's ideas for meeting deadlines but she agrees to do so because she's afraid she might get in trouble with her boss if she doesn't.

Were you able to identify the details that make this an example of success on Izzat's part at giving constructive criticism?

Single issue

It's clear that Izzat had focused on the single issue of timely reporting--in this case, the regional quarterly production reports.

Observable actions

Izzat carefully notes observable actions. She references Della's failure to gather the information she needs to complete the reports, which impedes her ability to get her work done on time.

Action plans

It's clear that Izzat is trying to get Della to discuss an action plan. This step is critical if Izzat is to be successful in providing constructive criticism to Della.

As you could tell, Nick had some problems to confront concerning his behavior. By following the methods you learned in this topic, you can provide constructive criticism to people like Nick.

In this topic, you learned to apply the appropriate methods for providing constructive criticism to someone in the workplace:
- focusing on the current issue,
- focusing on observable actions and behaviors,
- determining a plan of action.

SAYING NO RESPONSIBLY

Saying no responsibly

How often, after agreeing to something, have you reprimanded yourself with the question "Why didn't I just say no?"

In this topic, you'll learn about three guidelines for saying no responsibly to your co-workers or subordinates as you provide constructive feedback. You'll explore:
- knowing when to say no,
- knowing how to say no,
- providing alternatives.

It may sound contradictory, but when you can say no to others in a responsible way, you've discovered an important aspect of constructive feedback. Saying no responsibly is also a component of being an assertive business professional.

Saying no is part of constructive feedback because it allows you to stop the feedback recipient when his response is inappropriate or defensive. The first guideline is knowing when to say no--and realizing it at the time you should say it. Realizing you should have said no when you've already said yes isn't too helpful.

Misunderstandings

"I had to learn to say, 'No, you're not understanding; listen to me,' at times when it was clear a feedback recipient was not hearing my message."

Unwanted outcomes

"I also learned to say no in order to avoid undesirable outcomes. For example, I can say no to someone proposing an unrealistic goal during a feedback session."

The second guideline is knowing how to say no to others as you provide constructive feedback. You can whisper no in a passive way and you'll probably not be taken seriously by others. You can shout "No!" in an aggressive manner as you pound your desk, and you'll undoubtedly get your point across. But the best approach is to just say no in an assertive manner that is responsible and firm, and you'll be understood clearly without offending co-workers or employees.

Passive

Avoid being passive. Say no and expect others to believe you mean it. Be assertive by saying no in a calm but firm manner. People will respect you for taking a clear stand, especially if you justify or explain your negative response in a reasonable way.

Assertive

You can say the same word--no--and achieve widely different responses from people, depending on how you deliver the message. To get a positive, respectful response, just say no in an assertive manner.

Aggressive

Don't be overly aggressive and expect others to be enthusiastic about working with you. You'll find that saying no in an assertive way will strike a much better chord than an aggressive style.

Knowing how to say no assertively can help you stop an unproductive conversation and turn your feedback session to more constructive discussion--back to the direction you want the session to go.

There is a useful third guideline to saying no responsibly which involves providing alternatives. When you say no, you can suggest alternative approaches or actions whenever it's possible to do so. You'll foster a positive work environment when others see that you're taking a helpful approach, even when you have to say no.

Beth, a director, has the opportunity to practice saying no responsibly to Dan, a subordinate and supervisor in the power company's planning division. Follow along to observe how Beth provides alternatives to Dan's original request.

Dan: Beth, thanks for making the time to meet with me this afternoon.

Beth: That's OK. I realize you want a decision so you can move forward developing

Dan: Yes, I do. The planning staff is working at full capacity now--as I noted in my request to hire three more planners.

Beth: I realize that everyone on your staff is fully committed at the moment. However, I can't approve your request for new staff right now, given our budget situation.

Dan: I was afraid of that. I'm just not sure how to meet all the existing deadlines with the current planning group. I really hate asking for more overtime effort.

Assertive Communication

Beth: I have some ideas--and a positive decision--that I think will help resolve the situation.

Dan: Good. At the moment, it seems nothing has worked.

Beth: First, you can have Bill's help for two months to take over administrative tasks. And it's been decided to move the deadline back one month for the Newton project to allow you to focus on the new expansion plans.

Beth said no to Dan's request for staff. But she was able to provide alternatives by temporarily assigning a staff member to help out and by moving a deadline back to make time available for the new planning assignment.

Question

Before you can say no responsibly, it helps to understand the guidelines for doing so. Choose the guidelines for saying no responsibly as you provide constructive feedback to others.

Options

1. Provide alternatives after saying no.
2. Know how to say no to someone.
3. Know when to avoid saying no.
4. Know when to say no to someone.
5. Say no to avoid controversy.

Answers

Actually, saying no responsibly to someone as you provide constructive feedback involves knowing when and how to say no as well as providing alternatives after you say no.

Option 1: This option is correct. By providing alternatives, you foster a positive work environment when others see that you're taking a helpful approach, even when you have to say no. This is one of the guidelines to saying no responsibly.

Option 2: Correct. Another guideline to saying no responsibly is to know how to assertively say no to someone. By saying no in an assertive manner and firmly, you'll be understood clearly without offending co-workers or employees.

Option 3: This is an incorrect option. You should know exactly when to say no--and realize it at the time you should say it. Avoiding a no response creates problems and is not a guideline for saying no responsibly.

Option 4: Correct. Another guideline to saying no responsibly is knowing exactly when to say no--and realizing it at the time you should say it. Realizing you should have said no when you've already said yes isn't too helpful and creates problems.

Option 5: This is an incorrect option. Saying no helps you avoid undesirable outcomes, not controversy. Controversial topics will still require treatment.

You'll undoubtedly feel that your constructive feedback sessions are more manageable when you learn how to say no in a responsible manner. In this course, you learned about becoming more assertive professionally by using proactive listening and constructive feedback strategies in the workplace.

But you learned more than that. You learned that becoming an assertive business professional fosters your own growth as well as enables you to help co-workers and employees develop and grow.

CHAPTER II - ASSERTIVENESS FROM INSIDE TO OUTSIDE

CHAPTER II - Assertiveness from Inside to Outside
 SECTION I - Developing Your Assertive Style
 SECTION II - Self-development Strategies
 SECTION III - Assertive Interactions

SECTION I - DEVELOPING YOUR ASSERTIVE STYLE

SECTION I - Developing Your Assertive Style

You can take care of the future by assuming responsibility for changing your professional style. In this lesson, you'll learn about methods and guidelines that enable you to take the lead in becoming more assertive. You'll learn about:
- building your style,
- enhancing your style,
- strengthening your style,
- sharpening your style.

ACTION STRATEGIES FOR BEING AN ASSERTIVE BUSINESS PROFESSIONAL

Action strategies for being an assertive business professional

Many business journal articles suggest that assertive people exhibit the professional business style that dynamic, prosperous companies are seeking today--and that more companies will be seeking in the future.

Question

Have you fallen prey to the myth that the future takes care of itself? Are the given statements true or false?

You can't change your professional style. The workplace dictates your behavior. Change just happens; you can't plan for it.

Options:

1. true
2. false

Answer:

Actually, all three of these statements are myths about changing your personal style.

Option 1: These statements are not true. They claim that you have no control over your self, environment, or future. Actually, you can take care of all of these by assuming responsibility for them by changing your personal style.

Option 2: These statements are false because you can take care of the your future by assuming responsibility for developing your personal style. These statements falsely claim that you have no control over your self, environment, or future.

Think back to your most recent attempt to change your style. Even if you started the process in a positive frame of mind, you probably found it challenging and difficult. But the truth is that the results of going through the change process can be personally beneficial.

Improved self-image

Once you realize that you can effectively change your style, you're going to feel better about yourself. You'll also probably notice that you're willing to take on additional style changes because now you're more confident that you can be successful.

Improved relationships with others

Dealing either too passively or too aggressively with others can damage relationships. As you learn to be more assertive, you'll notice that relationships with co-workers, subordinates, and even higher-level supervisors can improve noticeably.

Enhanced capabilities

You will quickly realize that actions you take to change your style can result in observable enhancement of your personal and professional capabilities. This realization can increase your sense of well-being and intensify your desire to make further changes to your style.

Action strategies are your key to developing the assertive business style that will foster success, both today and in the future.

Question

What are the keys to success? Which statements describe benefits of learning action strategies for becoming an assertive business professional?

Options:

1. You can avoid confrontations with others.
2. You can develop your capabilities.
3. You can improve relationships with others.
4. You can reduce the number of negative traits.
5. You can enjoy a better self-image.

Answer:

Actually, benefits you can enjoy include improved self-image and relationships with others as well as enhancement of your capabilities.

Option 1: This option is not correct. Becoming an assertive business professional will not help you avoid confrontations with people, but it will make you more confident in difficult business situations.

Option 2: This is a correct choice. By realizing that your style changes result in observable enhancement of your capabilities, you increase both your sense of well-being and your desire to make further changes.

Option 3: This is a correct choice. The extremes of passive or aggressive behavior can damage relationships, but assertive behavior aids in building relationships. When you are assertive, your relations with others will improve noticeably.

Option 4: This choice is incorrect. You will not reduce the number of traits but you will learn how to change your behavior by becoming more assertive.

Option 5: Correct. As you learn action strategies to become more assertive, you'll realize that you can control changes in your life and you'll feel better about yourself, and about taking on additional changes as well.

BUILDING AN ASSERTIVE PROFESSIONAL STYLE

Building an assertive professional style

"You can't win them all, but you can sure lose them all." --Forde's second law

In this topic, you'll learn three strategies that are the foundation for building your assertive style. Once you're comfortable with these strategies, you can add additional elements to bolster your style. The strategies are:
- being proactive
- being accountable
- being an active participant.

Being proactive is a strategy you can employ to your personal advantage. Look for assignments where you can make a contribution and then volunteer to play a role. And seek a role that is responsible for a specific, measurable component of the project. After all, you want to receive credit for the work you accomplish.

You're also proactive when you anticipate future needs or issues and take steps to address them. Supervisors and co-workers alike will respond well when they realize the benefits of your actions and behavior.

Being accountable is another strategy that can help you build a more assertive style. You're being accountable when you personally ensure that you follow directions and carry out actions expected of you by others in the workplace.

Accountability also includes being answerable to others both for successes and problems when you have assumed a responsible role.

Lee has decided to be more accountable in carrying out his job assignments as a salesman for a software distributor. He believes that both his support staff and supervisor will notice and appreciate his newly assumed responsibility.

Lee 1

"I really focus on following directions and procedures. For example, now I always use the correct forms to report both my sales calls and actual sales."

Lee 2

"I ensure that my actions are in line with what's expected of me. I no longer waste valuable time, and I'm focused on meeting deadlines."

Lee is using an appropriate strategy for being accountable. He assumes personal responsibility for what is expected of him by others, and he wants others to recognize his new dedication. Being proactive and accountable are two strategies that will help you develop an assertive style. Being an active participant in your job is a third.

Active participation occurs when you take part in assignments or assume your share, or more, of the

Assertive Communication

workload. Marti, an entry-level manager at a wholesale food distributorship, is pursuing her goal of being a more active participant.

Assignments

"I don't wait for assignments to be given to me. I ask questions to discover what assignments are available, and then I request those I would like to be involved with. I think my supervisor likes the initiative that I'm demonstrating."

Sharing

"I make sure I carry my share of the workload in the office. I even take on additional work when I can and when it helps other managers complete important assignments. These are ways I demonstrate that I'm an active participant in essential activities."

Marti is using an appropriate strategy for achieving greater participation in her work assignments; she is seeking desired assignments and proactively offering to help other managers with essential work.

Jill and Kent, supervisors in a retail store's regional customer service center, discussed Kent's efforts to develop a role on a new project.

Jill: Hi, Kent. I'm glad you got the assignment you requested for the procedures project. Good for you.

Kent: Thanks. Asking for that assignment is part of my plan to be more proactive. And it worked: I told the managers what I could contribute to the project, and they agreed to put me on the team.

Jill: Great. I know you're an asset to the team. How's it been going? I know you've been working hard the past month or more.

Kent: I made a few suggestions for the project plan that were well-received. In fact, our manager told me that my ideas had really strengthened the plan.

Jill: Good. A good plan means that there's a better chance of doing a good job reviewing and revising the procedures you're looking at. What else have you been doing on the project?

Kent: I have responsibility for complaints from small-business customers. I've recommended a few key changes in the procedures that should cut our response time by at least 10 percent.

Jill: That's terrific. You seem to be doing well. No wonder you're pleased with your assignment.

Kent: Yes, I am. I'm being given the accountability for project assignments that I wanted. It's part of my strategy to develop a more assertive style.

How can you use strategies similar to those used by Kent to develop your own assertive style?

Question

You're laying the foundation for the style you want to develop. Match each strategy for building your style to the corresponding statement.

Options:

A. being proactive

B. being accountable

C. being an active participant

Targets:

1. I ensure that I do my share on every assignment.

2. I look for responsible roles that I can receive credit for doing well.

3. I make sure my actions are in line with accepted procedures.

Assertive Communication

Answer

It's important to understand how to use the methods taught in this topic: being proactive and accountable as well as being an active participant.

By doing your share on every assignment, you demonstrate that you have initiative and are willing to help wherever possible. This active participation contributes to your team and can enhance your professional capabilities.

By anticipating future needs and taking steps toward a lead role in addressing those needs, you are being proactive in a way that helps your team. This sort of visibility helps you receive credit where it's due.

You need to ensure that you're completing tasks as required and on time. By doing so, you establish a reputation of being accountable that will be recognized and appreciated by both your boss and your co-workers.

In this topic, you learned about three primary strategies for building your assertive professional style. These useful strategies encourage you to:

- be proactive,
- be accountable,
- be an active participant.

ENHANCING AN ASSERTIVE PROFESSIONAL STYLE

Enhancing an assertive professional style

Building a foundation for your assertive style is the starting point. As you become comfortable with your initial level of assertiveness, you'll find yourself asking what steps you can take to become even more assertive.

Well, just as you took the responsibility to develop your assertive style, you can also take the lead in enhancing that style.

Taking the lead is easier when you know you have something to help you, something to rely on when you're having a difficult time. In this topic, you'll learn about three primary guidelines--building blocks for enhancing your assertive style.

These guidelines are:
--Act decisively.
--Act loyally.
--Act credibly.

Max, a supervisor of a customer claims unit for an insurance company, is pursuing his goal of being a more assertive professional. He's following the first guideline by adopting a more decisive business demeanor. Max is decisive when he makes clear choices about when and how to act in business situations.

Max 1

"When a staff member has handled the customer poorly, I act decisively to identify the stage of the customer problem and the resolution required."

Max 2

"I also must determine how to act toward a subordinate in a difficult situation. And this decision can vary with each situation."

Max is determining when and how to act in a decisive manner, then following through with appropriate interventions with subordinates or customers.

Acting loyally is a second guideline for enhancing your style. There are two distinct ways you can exhibit loyalty in a business setting. First, you can play the role of loyal opposition by ensuring all options are presented.

Once a decision is made, however, you then need to be an active supporter of that decision in the workplace. Tim and Kate, concept designers for an advertising agency, discussed loyalty issues in a situation where they both disagreed with a design decision.

Tim: Well, Kate, I'd say we fought the good fight, but we lost. What would you say?

Kate: I'd say we were the loyal opposition. You know, like in the British parliament when they're having debates.

Tim: Good analogy. We certainly raised our concerns about the proposed direction of the ad campaign.

Kate: We sure did. And I thought we presented some really good alternative approaches.

Tim: Yes, we laid out all the options and made our recommendation. We just didn't convince the rest of the design team or the client manager.

Kate: Oh, well. It's not that the proposal is all that bad; it's just that I think it could have been a lot better.

Tim: Well, we can't have our way all the time. Maybe our ideas will prevail on the next ad campaign.

Kate: That's right. In the meantime, we need to get behind the decision and see what we can do to make it really work for the agency and the client.

Kate and Tim are acting loyally by presenting their alternatives and options to the design group and then accepting and actively supporting a decision that rejected their proposals for an advertising campaign.

Acting decisively and loyally are two ways to enhance your assertive style. Acting credibly is a third guideline to follow. When you're credible, others in the workplace will believe your words and actions.

Leah is focused on acting credibly. She believes that enhancing her credibility with her co-workers is an essential element of her desired assertive style.

Leah 1

"I'm believable when others think I'm truthful and the information I provide is as complete and accurate as I can make it."

Leah 2

"I enhance my trustworthiness when others believe I'll do what I say I will. My actions demonstrate my credibility."

Leah's focus on truthful communication, accurate information, and believable actions follows the third

Assertive Communication

guideline for enhancing her assertive style--acting credibly.

Question

You're prepared to be responsible for your professional style. Which are the guidelines for enhancing your style?

Options:

1. act loyally
2. act proactively
3. act reasonably
4. act credibly
5. act decisively

Answer

Actually, enhancing your assertive style requires you to act credibly, decisively, and loyally in workplace situations.

Option 1: This is a correct choice. By acting loyally, you ensure that all options are represented but that any decisions made, even if not what you would prefer, are supported.

Option 2: This choice is incorrect. Being seen as proactive is a benefit of an assertive style but not a guideline for enhancing your style. Three primary guidelines that would enhance your professional style are acting loyally, decisively, and credibly.

Option 3: This is an incorrect choice. While reasonableness is a good trait, it is not a way to enhance your assertive style. Assertiveness can be enhanced by being more decisive when the situation requires it.

Option 4: This is a correct choice. Acting credibly makes others believe in your words and actions. People believe that you are presenting accurate information and that you will do what you say you will, which adds strength to your style.

Option 5: This choice is correct. Acting decisively enhances your assertive style because your choices are clear and bring about immediate results with subordinates or customers.

Enhancing your assertive style beyond your established foundation can be satisfying. In this topic, you learned about three primary guidelines that can help you enhance your assertive style: Act decisively, act credibly, and act loyally in workplace situations.

SUCCESSFULLY STRENGTHENING AN ASSERTIVE STYLE

Successfully strengthening an assertive style
You're comfortable with the assertive style you've developed so far, and your co-workers recognize your accomplishments. In fact, you've been congratulated on your new style on a few occasions.

But your goal is to strengthen your style by assuming additional roles--roles that carry greater accountability and offer greater recognition for a job done successfully.

In this topic, you'll learn about the three primary roles you must play in strengthening your assertive style. You'll also learn how to play the roles in business situations. The roles are:
- problem solver,
- decision maker,
- rule maker.

Question
You may want to look beyond your immediate work unit and strengthen your style by seeking to play these roles in a wider setting, such as interdepartmental teams.

How comfortable do you feel in seeking out roles that offer greater accountability in a wider business setting?

Options:

1. not comfortable
2. unsure
3. comfortable

Answer

Regardless of your current comfort level, the assertive style you're developing will stand you in good stead as you move forward to assume additional roles.

These roles require you only to play an active part in the processes. It's not suggested that you must become a solo problem solver or decision maker.

Becoming a problem solver is the first role that can strengthen your assertive style. Actively seek situations where you can be involved in identifying problems and play a part in designing solutions.

Identify problems

Your assertive style is evident to others when you actively identify problems at an early stage, before they become major problems.

Offer viable options

As a problem solver, you're part of the solution when you offer viable options for addressing and resolving a problem.

Ruth, a nurse practitioner at a large urban clinic, is meeting with the internal medicine unit's patient-care team. Ruth has told the team members that her patients have been increasingly irritated about what they perceive as longer waits in the intake room before they see a health-care provider. Ruth has suggested that patients be told on their arrival if their appointment will occur on

Assertive Communication

time, and she's suggested that patients be given a reason if they face a delayed appointment.

In this situation, Ruth's next suggestion is to conduct a brief study to determine if patient wait time actually has increased. The proposed study will allow the team to take further action as suggested by the information gathered through the study.

Ruth has actively played the role of a problem solver. She identified a problem and suggested options for addressing and resolving it.

The role of decision maker is another role that can strengthen your assertive style. Seek situations where you can be involved in gathering vital information and offer informed opinions that will facilitate reaching a viable decision.

Bob, general manager for a large construction company, and Jim, an engineer, discussed a problem with a foreign-based client in the chemical industry.

Bob: Jim, what do you have on that problem we encountered in the approval process for our de-ethanizer tower design? We need to make a decision this week on how to proceed.

Jim: I've gathered quite a bit of information and some opinions from our in-country team. Both our lead design engineer and the on-site project manager believe that the design may not be the real issue.

Bob: That sounds problematic, and I'm not sure that I like it. What have you found out?

Jim: My information leads me to believe that the design issue is being used as camouflage. The information I received from other contacts confirms this.

Bob: What is the issue then? What is it we need to address?

Jim: In my opinion, the issue is our consulting contract. I believe our design will be approved if we add a subcontract clause and hire a local company in an advisory capacity.

Bob: We've certainly proceeded that way in other situations. Give me a memo proposing a subcontract, and we can pass it by our board and legal affairs office.

Jim: I'll do that. I imagine we can make a decision on the proposal and move forward soon.

The information that Jim gathered led him to develop an informed opinion that helped Bob make a decision. Can you think of situations where you can play a decision-making role?

A third role that can help you develop your assertive style is that of a rule maker. Seek situations where you can play an active role in establishing the policies and procedures that dictate how work is accomplished. You don't need to act as the final arbiter of the rules, but you do want to have input into the rule-making process, as Linda has discovered.

Linda volunteers to work on teams that will make recommendations to management about creating new policies and procedures and modifying or eliminating current ones. An important aspect of the rule-making role is to ensure that the rules are fair and that everyone involved understands them. Linda has definite ideas about fairness and clarity.

Fair

Assertive Communication

"I try to ensure that rules are fair to everyone involved. Other employees appreciate my efforts to bring fairness to the workplace."

Understandable

"I also make it my mission to see that rules are understandable to employees. That means no legalese or government regulation-type verbiage."

Question

Before you can strengthen your assertive style, you need to have a thorough understanding of the roles you can play. Based on what you just learned, select the primary roles involved in strengthening your style.

Options:

1. a performance-evaluation role
2. a decision-making role
3. a rule-making role
4. a negotiator role
5. a problem-solving role

Answer

Actually, strengthening your assertive style requires you to play three primary roles: problem solver, decision maker, and rule maker.

Option 1: This is an incorrect choice. While you may request studies or gather information to support more problem-solving or decision-making roles, a performance-evaluation role does not improve the chances of others seeing you as assertive.

Option 2: This is a correct choice because in a decision-making role, you gather vital information that you assemble or present in ways that inform important decisions.

Option 3: This choice is correct because in a rule-making role you will have direct impact on how things get done. By volunteering or seeking out ways to impact policies and procedures, you can be more assertive in dictating how work is accomplished.

Option 4: This is an incorrect choice. Acting in a negotiating role, although beneficial in its own way, will not demonstrate your ability be assertive. Participating in decision-making, problem-solving or rule-making is more assertive.

Option 5: This is a correct choice. Your assertive style is evident when you actively identify problems and propose solutions. This contribution toward positive solutions demonstrates an assertive attitude.

Now that you've practiced identifying the primary roles involved in strengthening your assertive style, you're ready to assess yourself.

Did I play a problem-solving role?

You should ask a lot of questions about this role. Did I play a part in identifying the problem? Did I help ensure that all aspects of the problem were understood? Did I proactively offer alternative solutions to the problem that was identified?

Did I play a decision-making role?

In this case, ask questions to determine if you had the input necessary for decision making to occur. Did I collect the essential information? Is the information reliable? Did I present informed opinions that would lead to effective decisions?

Did I play a rule-making role?

First, ask yourself if you're in a position to offer suggestions about policies and procedures. When you are,

Assertive Communication

ask questions such as: Did I do my part to achieve fairness in the rules? Have I ensured that everyone affected by the rules understands them?

Pam, a junior partner in a law firm, recently sent a memo to a managing partner. Pam has identified a problem with non profit assignments taking too much time for some junior partners. She believes this issue can be addressed by rotating assignments among more partners to spread the workload. Pam has gathered information from other partners and, in her opinion, the rotation approach addresses everyone's primary concerns about the amount of time spent on non profit assignments.

Finally, Pam has provided a suggestion for rewording the firm's current procedure for making non profit assignments to partners. The revision would spread these assignments among all the firm's midlevel and junior partners.

Pam successfully strengthened her assertive style. Were you able to identify the details that led to her success?

Problem solver

Pam carefully gathered information from the firm's other partners--those whose opinions would influence a decision. She also offered her opinion that a decision to rotate non profit assignments would meet with the partners' approval.

Decision maker

Pam's memo clearly identified non profit assignments as a problem. The memo also offered a reasonable option by suggesting that the assignments be rotated.

Rule maker

Pam's memo involved her in a rule-making role when she suggested specific revisions for the firm's internal procedure for making non profit assignments.

Case Study: Question 1 of 2

Scenario

When you play your roles well, others will benefit from your assertive actions. You'll be satisfied that you've taken the lead to strengthen your assertive style.

Question

Did Maria successfully play the roles necessary to strengthen her assertive style?

Options:

1. No, because although she played all three roles, she failed to provide sufficient information for the local agency director to make a viable decision regarding a waiver request.

2. Yes, because she addressed the problem, the federal government rules, and the decision that needed to be made by the local government agency in requesting a waiver.

3. No, because although she played the roles of problem solver and decision maker, she failed to play the role of rule maker by changing the local agency's rules for her department.

4. Yes, because she successfully played all three roles and made suggestions that would benefit both the local agency's clients and the employees.

Answer

Actually, Maria did play the roles of problem solver and decision maker but failed to play the role of rule maker because she failed to address the local agency's rules.

Assertive Communication

Option 1: This choice is incorrect. Maria did not play all three roles. She played the roles of problem solver and decision maker, but not of rule maker. In this case she did not address the local agency rules needed to comply with federal regulations.

Option 2: This option is incorrect. While Maria played the roles of problem solver and decision maker, she did not act as a rule maker because she did not address the local agency rules needed to comply with federal regulations.

Option 3: This is the correct choice. There are three roles necessary for strengthening one's assertive style. While Maria played two of those roles, she did not play the third role of rule-making.

Option 4: This option is incorrect because Maria did not play all three roles. She played the roles of problem solver and decision maker, but she failed to play the role of rule maker by changing the local agency's rules for her department.

Case Study: Question 2 of 2

What questions did you ask to assess if Maria successfully played the roles to strengthen her assertive style?

Options:
1. Has Maria played the role of rule maker?
2. Has Maria played the role of facilitator?
3. Has Maria played the role of team leader?
4. Has Maria played the role of decision maker?
5. Has Maria played the role of problem solver?

Answer

Actually, playing the roles of problem solver, decision maker, and rule maker can strengthen an assertive style.

Option 1: This is a correct choice. The role of rule-maker is one of the roles that strengthens an assertive style, so asking questions directly related to this goal accurately assess whether the role has been played.

Option 2: This option is incorrect. The role of facilitator is not one of the three roles for an assertive style, so this question will not effectively assess whether the three roles of decision-making, problem-solving or rule-making have been played.

Option 3: This option is incorrect. Being a team leader is not one of the roles that strengthen assertive style. One can play assertive roles without being a team leader, so this question does not accurately assess assertive roles.

Option 4: This is a correct option. This question determines if Maria had the input necessary for decision making to occur. Because decision-making is one of the roles that enhances an assertive style, this question assess that goal.

Option 5: This is a correct choice. Playing the role of a problem solver is one of the necessary roles for enhancing an assertive style, so this question will assess whether Maria is actually playing that role.

Think of business situations where you will be able to play these roles successfully, and envision yourself as an assertive business professional in those situations. In this topic, you learned that the three roles you can play to strengthen your assertive style are: problem solver, decision maker, and rule maker.

STRATEGIES TO USE FOR SHARPENING ONE'S ASSERTIVE STYLE

Strategies to use for sharpening one's assertive style

To best prepare for your future as an assertive business professional, you should learn from your past experiences in building, enhancing, and strengthening your assertive style.

In this topic, you'll learn strategies for being more visible and successful. They are essential for sharpening your assertive style. The strategies are:
- Assess how you demonstrate your assertive style.
- Modify your actions.
- Revise your assertiveness plan.

An initial strategy for sharpening your style is to conduct a self-assessment. That is, evaluate your style as you exhibit it in the workplace today. Susan, a benefits specialist in the human resources department of a major accounting and consulting firm, is relatively satisfied with the assertive style she's developed so far. But she believes there is more that she can do.

Decide what to assess

"First, I decided what to assess. I developed a checklist of the traits I display as a result of the steps I went through to build, enhance, and strengthen my style. I wanted to understand how I exhibit each trait in the workplace. That was my starting point."

Develop questions

"Then I developed questions to ask myself and others. Am I acting proactively? Am I being accountable? Am I decisive and credible? Am I playing assertive roles?"

Using the information

"Finally, I'm committed to using the information to revisit my original action plan and the objectives I set for myself. Based on the data, I can alter my plan and move assertively forward."

Susan is taking the lead again and being responsible for the ongoing development of her assertive style. She's assessing her past actions in order to better plan the next steps she wants to take to continue sharpening her style.

Question

Assessing how you're demonstrating your assertiveness is essential to planning the next steps in sharpening your style. According to the material just covered, how should you go about assessing your style?

Options:

1. I need to focus on those few specific assertiveness traits that are most important.

2. I need to design questions to ask myself that assess the specific assertiveness traits that I'm interested in.

3. I need to ask others, rather than myself, to assess how well I've done.

Assertive Communication

4. I need to decide exactly what it is about my style that I want to evaluate.

5. I need to actually review and use all the information that I've gathered.

Answer

Actually, you need to decide what to assess, develop questions to ask, and ensure that you follow through.

Option 1: This is an incorrect choice. As part of your assessment you should understand how you exhibit all traits in your work environment, not just a few traits.

Option 2: This option is correct. Questions on whether you're acting proactively, accountably or credibly, or whether you're playing an assertive role, will help you assess yourself in your new assertive style.

Option 3: This option is incorrect because you should be asking questions of yourself, although asking questions of others may be helpful as well.

Option 4: This choice is correct. Developing a list or checklist of what to watch for will help you focus your assessment and gather useful information.

Option 5: This option is correct. Using the information you've gathered allows you to implement necessary changes to your plan and objectives. Based on that data, you can alter your plan and move forward assertively.

You've taken actions in pursuit of your goal of being more assertive. Volunteering for a new team assignment or offering to take on additional duties in order to assist a co-worker are the types of actions you may have taken. You've also assessed your assertive style.

Once you've assessed your style, the next step is to modify your action plan. Of course, you modify your actions based on the answers to the questions you asked during the assessment of your current style.

From his assessment, Jeff determined some actions to add to his plan, and he also identified some actions to modify.

Add

"I don't need to stop any actions, but I do want to add a new one. I'm requesting a new assignment--with accountability-- on an interdepartmental project."

Modify

"I also want to modify an action.

I'd like to expand my current problem-solving role in the company and take on some additional issues."

After you assess your assertive style and modify your actions, the final step in sharpening your assertive style is to revise your assertiveness plan as needed. This action follows logically from assessing where you are now and modifying your planned actions. Revising your plan is the final step needed to complete the process of sharpening your assertive style.

Revise your milestones

Revise the milestones in your current plan, as needed, based on the assessment you conducted and any planned actions that you may have changed. Your milestones are periodic measurements of your progress as you develop your assertive style.

Revise your timetable

Your timetable helps you track how well you're following and maintaining your plan. Keep your timetable current so you can accurately monitor your progress. And revise your timetable if you've modified planned actions or revised your plan's milestones.

Assertive Communication

Schedule the next assessment

Finally, your plan should specify when your next self-assessment will occur. It's essential to periodically assess your assertive style. Use the results to modify planned actions and revise your plan.

Question

Everybody's plan needs to be revised from time to time. What are the steps in revising your assertiveness plan?

Options:

1. I may need to revise my timetable because of changes in my plan.

2. I need to schedule when to assess my assertive style next.

3. It may be necessary to revise future milestones because of assessment results.

4. I may need to rethink my goals and objectives based on the feedback I receive.

5. I'll need to decide if I am pursuing the correct traits to become an assertive person.

Answer:

Actually, your plan revision may need to include revising your milestones or your timetable as well as scheduling future assessments.

Option 1: This is a correct choice. Since a timetable helps you keep track of how well you're following and maintaining your plan, you should keep your timetable current as you revise your plan.

Option 2: This choice is correct. It is essential to periodically assess your assertive style and then use the results to modify planned actions and revise your plan.

Option 3: This is a correct choice. Because milestones are measurements of your progress, these will change over time as you develop your assertive style and need new or revised milestones.

Option 4: This option is incorrect. While you may revise your milestones, timetable, or specific actions based on your assessment, you will not need to entirely rethink your larger goals and objectives.

Option 5: This choice is incorrect. Deciding on traits for being assertive come well before you assess your strategic plan for how you are changing. At this point of assessing, you should be reviewing your timetable, milestones, and future assessment.

Once you've taken steps to prepare for the future, you're well-prepared to pursue and sharpen your desired assertive style.

Question

Sharpening your assertive style is an important step toward achieving your goal of being an assertive business professional. Which strategies can help you sharpen your assertive style?

Options:

1. Modify your style as needed to be in accord with your plan.

2. Modify your planned future actions in response to feedback you receive.

3. Follow a schedule to periodically assess your assertive style.

4. Follow your plan without deviation in order to achieve your goal.

5. Revise your plan for becoming an assertive person as needed.

Answer

Assertive Communication

Actually, preparing for the future involves assessing your assertive style, modifying future actions, and revising your assertiveness plan.

Option 1: This choice is incorrect. Your style should not be modified to align with your plan; rather, your plan supports your desired change in style. You should modify your plan and your actions in accord with your new assertive style.

Option 2: This is a correct choice. By modifying your planned future actions, you incorporate useful feedback or information and continue to sharpen your assertive skills.

Option 3: This choice is correct. It is essential to assess your assertive style at different points and then use the results of that assessment to modify planned actions and revise your plan.

Option 4: This is an incorrect choice. It is actually important to consider necessary revisions to your plan, including revising your timetable or milestones, based on information from your assessment.

Option 5: This is a correct choice. Information you gather in assessing your progress will help you see where you need to grow or have already grown. Based on that, you will need to revise your plan for on-going sharpening of your assertive style.

You can take action to further sharpen the assertive style that you've developed. In this topic, you learned about three strategies that can help you sharpen your style: assessing your assertive style, modifying your actions, and revising your assertiveness plan as needed.

SECTION II - SELF-DEVELOPMENT STRATEGIES

SECTION II - Self-development Strategies

In this lesson, you'll learn about taking the lead in using self-development strategies to achieve the assertive style you want.

The strategies that can guide you to success are:
--taking a positive approach,
--developing personal accountability.

THE VALUE OF LEARNING ASSERTIVE SELF-DEVELOPMENT STRATEGIES

The value of learning assertive self-development strategies

When you work to improve yourself, you reap the rewards. So take the lead in following self-development strategies that can help you build and strengthen the assertive style that's your desired goal.

The results of your actions can be rewarding. The strategies you'll learn in this lesson will help you know which actions to take to become more assertive. Sandra has realized the value of pursuing these strategies.

Attitude

"I saw my attitude about myself improve noticeably once I took charge and followed the self-development strategies. From comments I receive, I know others recognize how my attitude has changed for the better as I became more positive and accountable."

Self-worth

"My feeling of self-worth increased once I became responsible for my growth and development. It felt like I developed into the positive, accountable person I always wanted to be but had never quite been--until now."

Sandra has learned a valuable lesson. She's assumed full responsibility for her development, knowing that her actions will bring the reward she's seeking--a more assertive style.

Question

Taking charge of your self-development puts you in a position of strength. Given what you just learned, select the choice that describes the value of learning self-development strategies for being an assertive business professional.

Options:

1. enhanced self-worth and reduced aggressive behavior
2. improved personal capabilities and reduced aggression
3. enhanced self-worth and an improved professional attitude
4. less passive behavior and an improved professional attitude

Answer

Actually, the value of learning self-development strategies includes enhanced self-worth and an improved professional attitude.

Option 1: This is an incorrect choice. While enhanced self-worth is one of the values, the other value in self-development is an improved attitude that is more positive and accountable.

Option 2: This is an incorrect choice. Neither of these are the value in taking charge of your self-development. The value comes in a positive attitude about yourself and

Assertive Communication

a feeling of self-worth. The actions you take will then lead to improvements.

Option 3: This is the correct choice. The rewards you reap by taking charge of your self-development are blossoming into the person you always wanted to be and a better attitude about yourself.

Option 4: This is an incorrect choice. One of the values is having a better professional attitude, but less passive behavior is not a value. The other value is enhanced self-worth. Together, these may lead you to less passive behavior.

Go ahead and take charge of your life. Develop the professional style you've wanted, and display it to others at work and elsewhere.

METHODS FOR TAKING A POSITIVE APPROACH

Methods for taking a positive approach

By definition, a self-development strategy requires you to take the lead. And you can achieve the best results when you take a positive approach, which helps ensure that you'll succeed in becoming more assertive.

In this topic, you'll learn about three methods for taking a positive approach. These methods, which provide essential support for developing your assertive style, are:
- developing a positive attitude,
- acknowledging personal strengths,
- celebrating successes.

The first method might seem obvious: Develop a positive attitude. Your attitude is the key to building and strengthening the assertive style you want to claim as your own.

Les is focused on developing a positive attitude, an essential element of his desired assertive style.

Self-confidence

"I look for opportunities to build my self-confidence. I do this by seeking challenging assignments and those in which I know there's a good chance to be successful."
Self-worth
"I also focus on acknowledging my self-worth by recognizing the value that I contribute to the company and my co-workers."

Les is developing the positive attitude that is one pillar of the positive approach to becoming assertive. Another pillar of the positive-approach method is to acknowledge your personal strengths. Your positive attitude will enhance your ability to recognize and acknowledge those strengths.

Molly, a manager of a health club, is pursuing her goal of being more assertive. To that end, Molly is identifying her strengths and recognizing each one as a strength that contributes to her success as an assertive person.
Identification
"I've been developing a list of my strengths and I was surprised at how many I have. For example, I consider my positive attitude a personal strength and so do co-workers who appreciate my positive disposition."
Affirmation
"I have a lot of ways to recognize my strengths. For example, I actually post notes in conspicuous places--each note is a reminder of some strength. I find it important to constantly tell myself that I can use my strengths to foster my own success."
Accountability
"I think that another real strength in my particular job environment is my acceptance of accountability for the

work I do. My supervisor appreciates the fact that I'm responsible and accomplish what I say I will."

Would you find it useful to emulate Molly's actions to identify and recognize her personal strengths? Why or why not?

Celebrating successes is the third pillar of taking a positive approach to becoming more assertive. Go ahead and celebrate when you are successful in some endeavor. And don't forget to celebrate when you are part of a successful group.

Individual

"Large or small, I've learned to celebrate the successes I have at work. Having a massage is one way I like to celebrate and acknowledge that I did well."

Group

"I encourage any successful group that I'm part of to celebrate its success. It may be only bringing in a cake or going to lunch, but celebrations are important."

Question

Your use of self-development strategies can enhance the likelihood of your success on the job. Match each method for taking a positive approach with the corresponding statement.

Options:

A. Develop a positive attitude.
B. Acknowledge personal strengths.
C. Celebrate successes.

Targets:

1. An ability to empathize with others helps me in my job.
2. I'm looking for an assignment that will be a challenge.

Assertive Communication

3. I just bought a book that I've been wanting to read.
Answer

Actually, taking a positive approach involves developing a positive attitude and acknowledging your personal strengths as well as celebrating successes.

By identifying what you do well and how it contributes to the workplace, you are acknowledging your personal strengths. In doing so, you can focus on what you do well and contribute more of that.

By seeking assignments that challenge you, you are looking for opportunities to build your self confidence. This provides you both opportunities to succeed and develop a positive attitude about yourself and your work.

Meeting goals, large or small, is important and should be celebrated. These successes contribute to a more positive approach and help you be more assertive. Any success should be noted and celebrated.

In this topic, you learned that a positive approach will do wonders for you as you implement your self-development strategies to become a more assertive business professional.

The useful methods of the positive approach encourage you to:
--develop a positive attitude,
--acknowledge personal strengths,
--celebrate successes.

DEVELOPING ACCOUNTABILITY

Developing accountability
Personal accountability is illustrated by your willingness to be held responsible and to answer to others for your actions and behavior in the workplace. Personal accountability is a key to the assertive style you're developing. How do you feel about your level of accountability right now?

In this topic, you'll learn about the three elements of developing personal accountability. You'll also see examples and learn how to discern those elements in a variety of business situations. The elements are:
- acknowledging positive feedback,
- accepting constructive criticism,
- dealing with unwarranted criticism.

Learning to acknowledge positive feedback and use it to your advantage is an important element in developing personal accountability. When you're acting in an assertive style, acknowledging feedback includes being receptive and giving appropriate feedback.

Aknowledgement

Assertive Communication

"I make it a point to acknowledge positive feedback. I let Veta know that I hear what she's saying, and I tell her that I appreciate her thoughtful remarks."

Feedback

"I give feedback too. I let her know how her contribution made me successful or tell her about her actions and behaviors that have a positive effect on others."

Remember that it's OK to accept and acknowledge positive feedback from others. Use the feedback to enhance your self-confidence and contribute in a positive way to the development of your assertive style.

Another element in developing personal accountability is learning to accept constructive criticism in a work situation. Accept it in the same professional way that you accept positive feedback.

Constructive criticism is intended to help you develop professionally. At times, such criticism may be received in conjunction with positive feedback, especially when coming from your supervisor. You take a big step forward when you learn to accept constructive criticism and learn from it.

Accept it well

Accept constructive criticism in a positive manner by being attentive and receptive. Remember that, by definition, the criticism is being given to you by someone who wants you to grow and be successful.

Learn from it

It's important that you listen to and hear the criticism so you can learn from it. Accepting constructive criticism should help you learn and grow professionally.

Learning to deal with unwarranted criticism is the third element you can use to develop personal accountability.

You've undoubtedly been in situations where you received unwarranted criticism. How well did you deal with the criticism? Consider Karen's situation: She's an attorney in a large law firm and is responding to undeserved criticism.

Confront

"I confronted the criticism by saying that I knew it wasn't warranted based on anything I'd done or said. I'm assertive in never letting criticism go unanswered."

Refute

"I refuted the criticism with facts. I didn't let the issue become personal, but I didn't allow myself to be overwhelmed by criticism that I knew I didn't deserve."

Question

Karen acted assertively in rejecting unwarranted criticism. To act otherwise could be harmful to her and give others the impression that the criticism was justified.

Think back on a workplace situation in which you were the recipient of criticism that you didn't deserve. How assertive were you in refuting that unwarranted criticism?

Options:

1. not assertive
2. somewhat assertive
3. don't really know
4. assertive
5. very assertive

Answer

Regardless of how you rated yourself, you can serve yourself well by learning to confront and refute unwarranted criticism.

Assertive Communication

Question

You want to work with others, and personal accountability shows others that you are responsible. What are the primary elements of developing accountability?

Options:

1. accepting constructive criticism
2. acknowledging positive feedback
3. dealing with personal assessments
4. accepting credible rewards
5. dealing with unwarranted criticism

Answer

Actually, developing personal accountability involves three elements: accepting positive feedback and constructive criticism as well as dealing with unwarranted criticism.

Option 1: This is a correct choice. Constructive criticism is intended to help you develop personal accountability, so accepting it is a way of taking responsibility both for your actions and your growth.

Option 2: This choice is correct. Acknowledging feedback shows that you have heard what another person is telling you, and that you appreciate the opportunity to learn and grow.

Option 3: This choice is incorrect. Personal assessment is an individual activity. Personal accountability is illustrated by your willingness to be held responsible and to answer to others for your actions and behavior in the workplace.

Option 4: This is an incorrect choice. Developing personal accountability means accepting critical feedback and thoughtful remarks about how you can improve, not accepting rewards for work done well.

Option 5: This is a correct choice. Being personally accountable is knowing when the criticism is fair and when it is not. When you are assertive, you won't allow yourself to be bothered by unwarranted criticism and will refute it with facts.

Now that you've learned about the primary elements involved in developing personal accountability, you're ready to assess whether you're actually using the elements.

Did I accept positive feedback?

When you're accepting positive feedback, be sure that you're acknowledging it so the giver knows you've actually heard it. And be sure to give positive feedback in return if it's reasonable to do so. If reciprocity fits the situation, use it.

Did I accept constructive criticism?

Accepting constructive criticism can help you greatly. Be sure to accept it in a positive, appreciative manner. And then take the all-important next step--make sure that you learn from the criticism and change your behavior, if necessary.

Did I deal with unwarranted criticism?

Remember that you shouldn't accept criticism that's unwarranted. Always confront such criticism, and firmly refute it by using facts and observable actions.

Dan and Jack are co-workers in a brokerage house in a large Eastern city. Dan talked to Jack about his handling of a client's account.

Dan: You did a good job handling the Patterson account. He can be a difficult client to deal with.

Assertive Communication

Jack: Thanks for the compliment. Actually, your coaching on dealing with difficult clients really set me up for success on this account.

Dan: I'm glad I could help. If you'd like more advice, I noticed you didn't suggest tax-deferred municipal bonds. I'd recommend that you always offer the full range of options to him.

Jack: That's a good point. And you're right. I didn't think he would be interested in municipal bonds. In the future, I'll offer the options and let him decide.

Dan: I also heard that you had an argument with Mr. Patterson. Remember that you need to be really careful in the way you treat our clients.

Jack: You must have heard that from Chad in the next office. Actually, we didn't have an argument. He expressed some thoughts on current politics rather loudly, but that had nothing to do with our business.

Dan: That sounds like Patterson. He does get excitable when he talks about politics. I'm glad there wasn't a problem.

Were you able to identify the details that demonstrated Jack's personal accountability?

Jack 1

Jack accepted Dan's positive feedback and returned the compliment. He also accepted the criticism and noted how he would act differently in the future.

Jack 2

Jack also confronted and rejected the undeserved criticism. His facts convinced Dan that the criticism was not warranted in this case.

Case Study: Question 1 of 2
Scenario

Kevin is a training manager for a cable company. He has 20 years of experience in training and has been the manager for five years. Kevin has reviewed the division managers' assessments of an innovative training program he put in place last year. In his response to the managers, Kevin thanks them for their support and their positive comments. Kevin is acknowledging the less-than-enthusiastic reception of the budgeting modules and is announcing plans to revamp those modules based on the comments received from managers and trainees. Kevin rejects the complaint that the training is too long; in fact, he's providing trainee-generated data approving the program's length and depth. He's also providing data indicating that supervisors who've completed the training are more efficient and effective. Overall, Kevin is pleased with his program and the response to it from others in the company.

Decide whether Kevin used the elements to develop personal accountability by answering the questions in order.

Question

Was Kevin successful in using the elements to develop personal accountability?

Options:

1. Yes, because he thanked managers for their comments, accepted criticism of the training program's length, and is planning changes to meet the criticism.

2. No, because although he accepted criticism and is planning changes, he didn't announce how he would make program changes.

Assertive Communication

3. Yes, because he thanked managers for their comments, accepted criticism of the budgeting modules and plan

changes, and refuted unwarranted criticism.

4. No, because although he thanked managers for their comments and confronted unwarranted criticism, he didn't refute the criticism of the budgeting modules.

Answer

Actually, Kevin used the elements of accepting both positive feedback and constructive criticism, and he dealt with the unwarranted criticism of the training program.

Option 1: This choice is incorrect because Kevin did not refute unwarranted criticism but instead accepted it, instead he allowed himself to be forced into taking unnecessary blame.

Option 2: This choice is incorrect because Kevin did include comments on how he plans to revamp the training based on feedback from managers and trainees.

Option 3: This is the correct choice. Kevin was appreciative of the feedback he received and accepted the comments that were helpful but refuted claims that he had data to disprove.

Option 4: This is an incorrect choice. Kevin did refute the unwarranted criticisms by providing trainee-generated data on the module length and depth. He also provided data on supervisors' improvement after the training.

Case Study: Question 2 of 2

What questions did you ask to assess if Kevin successfully used the elements to develop personal accountability?

Options:

1. Has Kevin dealt with unwarranted criticism?

2. Has Kevin accepted change suggestions?
3. Has Kevin accepted constructive criticism?
4. Has Kevin accepted positive feedback?
5. Has Kevin dealt with personality issues?

Answer

Actually, you need to ask if positive feedback and constructive criticism were accepted. You also need to ask if Kevin dealt with unwarranted criticism.

Option 1: This is a correct question. If Kevin is developing personal accountability, he will not allow himself to be overwhelmed by criticism without foundation. He will refute it to maintain his credibility and accountability.

Option 2: This is not a correct question. While Kevin may accept some change suggestions, there are others he should refute to develop accurate accountability.

Option 3: This is a correct question. By accepting constructive criticism, Kevin can determine how to grow and do a better job. This will help him become more accountable for the quality of his work.

Option 4: This is a correct question. Accepting positive feedback lets others know that Kevin hears what they say and that he appreciates the feedback they give that allows him to grow and learn.

Option 5: This is an incorrect choice. Personal accountability is a willingness to be held responsible and answer to others for actions and behavior.

Kevin did a good job of developing his personal accountability by using the three elements discussed in this topic. He was especially effective in dealing with the unwarranted criticism of his training program.

Assertive Communication

Personal accountability is a major factor in professional assertiveness. In this topic, you learned about three primary elements of developing accountability: accepting positive feedback, accepting constructive criticism, and dealing with unwarranted criticism.

SECTION III - ASSERTIVE INTERACTIONS

SECTION III - Assertive Interactions

You don't need to be nervous about dealing with others in work situations. In this lesson, you'll learn about methods and guidelines that enable you to work in a variety of interactive situations in an assertive professional manner. You'll learn about:
- developing a winning team style,
- negotiating effectively,
- establishing productive partnerships,
- dealing effectively with opposition.

INTERACTION STRATEGIES

Interaction strategies

Your immediate co-workers have commented positively about the difference they've seen in your professional style. You're feeling good about the changes you've made.

Then it happens: You're confronted with a situation involving a number of peers from different divisions within the company. You're nervous. How do you put your assertive style into action now?

Question

It's one thing to practice an assertive style with your immediate co-workers. But for many people it's more difficult to be assertive with an expanded group of professionals, especially those from other work units or outside the company.

How comfortable do you feel when you need to interact assertively with individuals outside your department?

Options:
1. not comfortable
2. unsure
3. comfortable

Answer

Regardless of your current comfort level, following interaction strategies will enable you to deal well with other professionals throughout the company--and beyond.

Exhibiting an assertive style can help you interact with a wide range of other business professionals, including co-workers, subordinates, and even your superiors in the organization.

Improved communication with peers

As you use interaction strategies, you'll find that communication with your peers improves. You'll be more direct in what you communicate and more attentive in hearing what's communicated to you. It's a win-win situation for all concerned.

Strengthened work relationships

You'll strengthen relationships with others once you implement interaction strategies. They will appreciate your assertive style and its results as you interact in team settings, negotiate successfully, or build effective partnerships.

Enhanced coping abilities

Interaction strategies can enable you to deal effectively with a variety of business situations. For example, these strategies will allow you to confront and cope with opposition in a professional manner.

Question

Using what you've learned, select the statements that describe benefits of learning interaction strategies to become an assertive professional in various business situations.

Options:

1. You can strengthen your work relationships.

2. You can enhance your coping abilities.
3. You can strengthen intergroup responsibilities.
4. You can improve communication with your peers.
5. You can enhance your stress management skills.

Answer

Actually, benefits of interaction strategies include improved communications, strengthened relationships, and enhanced coping abilities.

Option 1: This is a correct choice. Others will appreciate your assertive style and its results as you interact in team settings, negotiate successfully, or build effective partnerships.

Option 2: This choice is correct. These strategies will allow you to confront and cope with opposition in a professional manner in a variety of business situations.

Option 3: This is an incorrect choice. Interaction strategies will strengthen work relationships through improved communication, not intergroup responsibilities.

Option 4: This choice is correct. You'll be more direct in what you communicate and more attentive in hearing what's communicated to you. This creates a win-win situation for everyone.

Option 5: This choice is incorrect. Interaction strategies will help you improve your abilities to cope with different situations but it is not a stress management technique.

x

DEVELOPING A WINNING TEAM STYLE

Developing a winning team style

"Coming together is a beginning, staying together is progress, and working together is success." --Henry Ford, American industrialist

You can use your assertive approach to ensure that your team comes together and works together to develop a winning style that leads to success.

Most business professionals serve on teams at various times during their careers. In this topic, you'll learn about three primary steps to follow in developing a winning team style:

- clarifying your team's purpose,
- clarifying team roles,
- staying on task.

First, determine what the team is expected to do or accomplish. Be an assertive team member, and encourage your team to clarify its purpose before jumping into other team activities.

Assertive Communication

You should ask questions that will help clarify the team's purpose, such as: What exactly is our assignment? If that's our goal, do we know how to get there? Do we have ideas for an action plan?

Team member 1

"I raise questions in team discussions to ensure that everyone on my team agrees on the team's tasks and ultimate goal. That's essential to our success."

Team member 2

"I urge team members to clarify the strategy we'll use to achieve our goal during the initial phase of forming the team."

When your team's members reach agreement on the group's purpose, the group is ready to take the second step in setting the team up for success: clarifying team roles.

For your team to successfully follow its strategy and achieve its goal, make sure you clarify the roles various team members need to perform.

Identify team roles

Identify roles you and your team members need to fill. Decide what roles are essential to your success. Determine if roles should be permanent or if they should rotate among team members.

Clarify role responsibilities

Be assertive by ensuring that all team members are in agreement about the responsibilities of each team role. Take the time to brainstorm lists of responsibilities. This step helps guarantee that no responsibility is overlooked.

Assign team roles

Request the role you want to play, and encourage others to do the same. Encourage team members to take individual strengths into account as roles are assigned. Place team members in roles where they can be successful.

Question

Ensuring that team roles are appropriately defined and assigned is an important part of setting up the team for success. What are the elements of the second step--clarifying team roles?

Options:

1. clarifying the responsibilities of each role
2. clarifying the team's goals and strategies
3. identifying the necessary team roles
4. identifying the team's schedule
5. assigning roles to individual team members

Answer

Actually, clarifying the team's roles involves identifying necessary roles, clarifying the responsibilities of each role, and then assigning roles to team members.

Option 1: This is a correct choice. Team members should be clear on each role and in agreement about the responsibilities of those roles. This guarantees that responsibility is not overlooked.

Option 2: This is an incorrect choice. A winning team style requires identifying team roles, not goals and strategies. Goals and strategies will be determined by actions not related to style.

Option 3: This choice is correct. It is important to determine what roles are essential to success. The team should also determine what roles may be permanent or rotating.

Option 4: This choice is incorrect because a winning team style focuses on roles for success within the team, not

Assertive Communication

a specific schedule. The schedule will be determined for the team to succeed in managing the project well.

Option 5: This is a correct choice. Assigning team roles takes into account individual strengths and preferences for opportunities to grow. This part of developing a winning team style ensures success of the team.

Whenever team members are planning activities, remind them to stop and ask themselves if their plans are in line with company strategies and if they will contribute to reaching company goals. This keeps them on track and helps them avoid wasted time and effort. "Focus on the goal" is the mantra to repeat to team members.

When you play your role well, your team members are efficient and effective as they work toward the team's goal.

Question

Your team can be a winning team with the appropriate effort. Which are the steps for developing a winning team style?

Options:

1. Identify the pitfalls the team faces on a daily basis.

2. Ensure that team members stay focused and on task.

3. Clarify the roles that team members need to create and fill.

4. Ensure that team members are from the same department.

5. Clarify the team's purpose--the reason the team exists.

Answer

Actually, developing a winning team style requires you to clarify the team's purpose and roles and stay on task.

Option 1: This is an incorrect choice. Steps to a winning team style include clarifying team roles, clarifying the team's purpose, and ensuring that members stay on task.

Option 2: This is a correct choice. To avoid wasted time and effort, the team should stop and ask themselves if their plans are in line with company strategies and if they will contribute to reaching company goals.

Option 3: This choice is correct. By clarifying the roles, your team ensures that no responsibility is overlooked. It also ensures that all team members are aware of the roles and in agreement about each role's responsibilities.

Option 4: Incorrect. Team members don't have to be from the same department. The team should decide what roles are important to be successful and fill them based on their criteria. This may require team members to be from other departments.

Option 5: This is a correct choice. The team's purpose should be determined before any activities are undertaken. Clarifying the team's purpose includes having a clear goal and strategy.

Whether as a team member or team lead, you can use an assertive approach to help develop an effective team style. In this topic, you learned that clarifying your team's purpose, clarifying team roles, and staying on task are the steps to follow to achieve team success.

SUCCESSFUL NEGOTIATIONS

Successful negotiations

"Like it or not, you are a negotiator. Negotiation is a fact of life." --Roger Fisher and William Ury, Harvard University professors

Question

If you're a business professional, you negotiate as part of your job. For large issues and small issues alike, negotiation occurs constantly in business situations.

Are you comfortable when you're the negotiator in a business setting?

Options:

1. not at all well
2. not too well
3. unsure
4. well
5. very well

Answer

Regardless of how you rated yourself at this time, you can benefit immensely by learning the primary steps to successful negotiation.

Negotiation skills don't come naturally--they're usually learned. But once you've learned them, you'll be comfortable in the various situations that require you to negotiate with other business professionals.

In this topic, you'll learn about three steps for successful negotiation. These steps are:
- clarifying objectives,
- offering reasonable propositions,
- compromising effectively.

The first step of successful negotiation is to clarify your objectives and those of the other party. You need to understand your objectives before entering into a bargaining session, and you must be able to clearly state them to the opposition. Then you need to ask pointed questions that will elicit clear identification of the other party's objectives during the opening phase of the negotiation.

Clark, an insurance company manager, is following the second step for successful negotiation: offering reasonable propositions that address both his company's interests and the interests of the insured employee group on the other side of the bargaining table.

Clark 1

"I'm offering a settlement that adheres to the policy's monetary cap of $1 million. That meets my company's requirement to follow standard industry practices."

Clark 2

"In line with your request, we consider your group's attorney's fees as a separate issue under the negotiation guidelines we established earlier."

Clark is taking what he views as a reasonable approach to the negotiations by following normal insurance

Assertive Communication

standards and offering to honor the employee group's request concerning attorney's fees. The third step in working toward the successful close of a negotiation is to compromise effectively.

Compromising is often required for negotiations to conclude successfully. In the beginning, the two parties usually set objectives that represent a win for them. The art of compromise alters those objectives until each side believes it has gained the most it can hope to gain while losing the least it can afford to lose. In the end, compromising effectively results from offering viable alternatives to your original position and requesting the same from the other side.

Compromise 1
"I offer concessions in incremental steps because I don't want to offer more than is needed. Yet I know I must offer something to move the negotiations away from the starting point, where each side asks for its ideal objectives."

Compromise 2
"You can't be bashful in asking the other side to revise its position. Ask for what you need in order to move the negotiations forward to a successful conclusion."

Question
You know you will be involved in some form of negotiation in the workplace, and you want to be successful. What steps should you follow to achieve successful negotiations?

Options:
1. offer reasonable propositions
2. compromise effectively
3. know when to go on the offensive

4. clarify everyone's objectives

5. seek the winning advantage

Answer

Actually, the essential steps to successful negotiation are clarifying objectives, offering reasonable propositions, and compromising effectively.

Option 1: This is a correct choice. Reasonable propositions address the interests of all parties involved to make successful negotiation possible.

Option 2: This choice is correct. Effective compromises allow each side to gain the most it can hope to gain but lose the least it can afford to lose. Effective compromises are viable alternative to the original positions presented.

Option 3: This choice is incorrect. Successful negotiation includes understanding and incorporating the other party's objectives and interest, not enforcing your own without compromise. Successful negotiation will require some concessions.

Option 4: This choice is correct. To begin successful negotiation, you must first have a clear understanding of your company's objectives and interests. You must also gain understanding of the other party's interests so you can move forward.

Option 5: This is an incorrect choice. The winning position is one where everyone gains the most and loses the least. Successful negotiation is determining how to make that happen, not how to win for just your company.

You've learned about the steps involved in negotiating successfully. Now you're ready to assess yourself.

Did I clarify objectives?

When you begin a negotiation, it's imperative that you clarify objectives--both yours and those of the other side.

Assertive Communication

If you fail to do so, you can find yourself confused and going nowhere in the discussion.

Did I offer reasonable propositions?

Ask yourself if you have offered reasonable propositions. Remember that the key word is "reasonable," as defined by both sides of the bargaining table.

Did I compromise effectively?

Compromising effectively requires treading a fine line. You need to offer alternatives when the bargaining falters. And you need to ask the people on the other side to reconsider their offer when they pose a roadblock to reaching a solution.

Amy is negotiating with a government agency. In an opening statement, she presented a detailed explanation of her company's request for a waiver of regulations. Then she asked questions to determine the opening stance of the government representatives. Amy later asked the agency to revise its position by granting her company a two-year waiver to allow time to take steps to meet required standards.

She explained that the waiver would allow the company to make changes to plant equipment and be exempt from fines during that period. As a final alternative, she suggested that changes could be made under a one-year waiver if federal funds were made available to mitigate the costs.

Were you able to identify the details that make this an example of a successful negotiation?

Select each factor, in order, for more information.

objectives

Amy was clear in detailing her company's objective: a waiver of regulations administered by the government agency. She also asked questions to clarify the agency's objectives.

propositions

Amy offered reasonable propositions. First, she proposed that the regulation in question be waived for a two-year period to allow the industry to make necessary alterations to equipment. Later she asked for a one-year waiver accompanied by federal funding.

compromises

Amy compromised effectively, revising her offers and asking the agency to do so as well. The two sides agreed to a one-year waiver accompanied by federal funds to offset the increased costs.

Amy followed all the guidelines for successful negotiation--clearly stated objectives, reasonable propositions, and effective compromise.

Case Study: Question 1 of 2

Scenario

Bradley, a reporter for a local newspaper, was negotiating with Edward, the news director. They were working out reporters' assignments for the coming year. Bradley told Edward that he wants more interesting stories to cover and report. If given his choice, Bradley would like to cover the government house and the political scene. By asking questions, Bradley discovered that Edward's goal was to change reporters' assignments on an incremental basis. In response, Bradley suggested a few options, including dividing the government house assignment with the current political reporter who would get the news stories of her choice. He also suggested

Assertive Communication

another alternative: doing some of the crime scene reporting. Of course, Bradley asked Edward to reconsider his reluctance to change assignments more often.

Evaluate Bradley's negotiation with Edward by answering the questions in order.

Question

Did Bradley correctly follow the steps necessary for successful negotiation with his news director?

Options:

1. No, because although Bradley clarified his objectives, he didn't take Edward's objective into account, and he failed to offer options that Edward would view as reasonable.

2. Yes, because Bradley clarified both Edward's and his own objectives, and he offered reasonable propositions and compromise positions on his requested reporting assignment.

3. No, because Bradley wasn't specific in what he meant by covering more interesting stories, and he didn't offer a compromise request that wouldn't affect other reporters.

4. Yes, because Bradley clarified his desired assignment and offered reasonable alternatives to Edward's incremental approach and reluctance to change the political assignments.

Answer

Actually, the basics of negotiation include clarifying objectives, offering reasonable propositions, and compromising effectively.

Option 1: This is an incorrect choice. Bradley modified his original suggestion to incorporate Edward's goals and suggested a second alternative that balanced his objectives with Edward's.

Option 2: This is the correct choice. Bradley both presented his side and listened to Edward's side. After hearing Edward, Bradley came up with specific recommendations that suited both their objectives.

Option 3: This is an incorrect choice. Bradley specified that he wanted government house and political science stories. When he adapted his suggestion to reach a compromise, he specifically offered to let the senior reporter have her choice of stories.

Option 4: This is an incorrect choice. Bradley went further than this: he clarified Edward's objectives as well and modified his suggestions to incorporate Edward's needs. This allowed for a compromise to be reached.

Case Study: Question 2 of 2

What questions did you ask to assess if Bradley followed the steps for successful negotiation?

Options:

1. Was Bradley making proactive requests?
2. Was Bradley suggesting effective compromises?
3. Was Bradley offering reasonable propositions?
4. Was Bradley arguing his cause effectively?
5. Was Bradley clarifying the relevant objectives?

Answer

Actually, clarifying objectives, as well as suggesting reasonable propositions and effective compromises, are essential to effective negotiation.

Option 1: This is an incorrect choice. One of the steps is offering reasonable propositions that consider all parties' interests, not just proactive requests that represent one party's interest.

Option 2: This is a correct choice. This question focuses on one of the three steps for successful negotiation.

Assertive Communication

Suggesting effective compromises helps every party involved gain the most and lose the least.

Option 3: This is a correct choice. You should assess whether both sides of the bargaining table are represented in the proposed compromises.

Option 4: This is an incorrect choice. It is imperative to understand both sides of the case. Otherwise, discussions may reach a dead end and fail to compromise and move forward.

Option 5: This is a correct choice. Clarifying the objectives for all interested parties allows the process of negotiation to take place. Failure to do so could stall discussions because one or both parties is being neglected.

Do you think you can be as successful at negotiating as Bradley was? In this topic, you learned to assess the use of three steps for successful negotiations. You are negotiating effectively when you:

- clarify objectives,
- offer reasonable propositions,
- compromise reasonably.

ESTABLISHING A PRODUCTIVE PARTNERSHIP

Establishing a productive partnership

Orville and Wilbur Wright's partnership helped them get off the ground. Partnerships can be a productive part of your professional life too.

Have you wondered about how to develop a productive partnership? The steps in this topic can help you establish winning partnerships.

In this topic, you'll learn three steps for establishing a productive partnership: identifying common goals, establishing each partner's responsibilities, and recognizing the need to celebrate accomplishments.

Question

Developing the right partnerships with the right people can be a big factor in your success. How do you feel about establishing partnerships? Is it something you're comfortable with?

Options:

1. not at all likely
2. unlikely

3. uncertain
4. likely
5. very likely

Answer

Option 1: If you're not likely to jump at the opportunity, you'll be glad to know there are proven methods to help you. If you're on the positive end of the scale, you'll find these methods will help you move into a partnership with greater ease and speed.

Option 2: If you're not likely to jump at the opportunity, you'll be glad to know there are proven methods to help you. If you're on the positive end of the scale, you'll find these methods will help you move into a partnership with greater ease and speed.

Option 3: If you're not likely to jump at the opportunity, you'll be glad to know there are proven methods to help you. If you're on the positive end of the scale, you'll find these methods will help you move into a partnership with greater ease and speed.

Option 4: If you're not likely to jump at the opportunity, you'll be glad to know there are proven methods to help you. If you're on the positive end of the scale, you'll find these methods will help you move into a partnership with greater ease and speed.

Option 5: If you're not likely to jump at the opportunity, you'll be glad to know there are proven methods to help you. If you're on the positive end of the scale, you'll find these methods will help you move into a partnership with greater ease and speed.

Truly productive associations seldom happen by chance; more commonly, they happen by design. Unlike teams, to which members are usually assigned, a partnership is something you seek to establish because you see a real benefit to working with someone else. And unlike coaches, who are also often assigned, a partner will agree to work with you because he can see a benefit to doing so.

Identify common goals

You initiate a partnership by identifying common goals that the partners want to reach. It's a good idea to make sure that everyone is in agreement on this important step before moving on to other aspects of the partnership.

Establish each partner's responsibilities

Next, ask what each partner will do to make the partnership a success. That's an important question you need to answer early because the success of your partnership depends on everyone knowing his part and playing that part responsibly.

Recognize the need to celebrate accomplishments

You and your partners will want to celebrate your accomplishments. You can recognize this need by planning celebrations around milestones you reach. And definitely plan a celebration for when you achieve your partnership's final goal.

Question

Partnerships require time and effort to establish, but the payoff of a productive partnership can be incalculable. From the information you just learned, what are the primary methods for establishing a productive partnership?

Options:

1. Be certain your time frame is all-inclusive.
2. Recognize the need to celebrate accomplishments.

Assertive Communication

3. Take time to identify common goals.
4. Take steps to develop common interests.
5. Be certain to establish each partner's responsibilities.

Answer

Actually, a productive partnership is built around common goals and well-defined responsibilities plus the need to recognize when a celebration is appropriate.

Option 1: This is an incorrect choice. Establishing a partnership focuses on common goals, clear responsibilities, and recognition of accomplishments. Time frames are not addressed while a partnership is being established.

Option 2: This is a correct choice. Celebrations can be organized around important milestones and are an important way of recognizing what's been accomplished and the overall value of the partnership.

Option 3: This choice is correct. It is important to make sure that everyone is in agreement on the goals before moving on to other aspects of the partnership.

Option 4: This choice is incorrect. While one step is to identify common goals, common interests are a precursor to actively establishing a partnership. Common interests are what often lead people to see the value in a potential partnership.

Option 5: This is a correct choice. Establishing responsibilities makes it clear what each partner will do to reach success. The success of your partnership hinges on everyone knowing his part and playing that part responsibly.

Catherine, a laboratory manager in a university hospital, sees an opportunity to establish a partnership with Dr. Davis, the director of medical research projects.

She thinks that a revision of existing forms and procedures for submitting samples for analysis and returning results would benefit both her laboratory technicians and the medical researchers.

Present idea

"I like my idea for revising forms and procedures--a very desirable goal for me. But what will Dr. Davis think? I need to present my idea to him with a rationale for forming a partnership around what I hope he'll see as a common goal."

Reach agreement

"If Dr. Davis agrees with my initial idea, we then need to meet and hash out the details. We need to reach agreement on our common goal and the rationale behind it so we can present similar information to our staff members."

What do you think about Catherine's plan to approach Dr. Davis to ask about working together? Is there something you can learn from Catherine's style that will make you more likely to take the chance to establish a partnership with someone in your own work environment?

Catherine and Dr. Davis will need time to meet and fill in the details of any partnership agreement they reach. That includes establishing the responsibilities that each of them will fulfill.

You and your partners will need to follow in the footsteps of Catherine and Dr. Davis. In their case, they brainstormed a list of responsibilities they thought their collaboration required. Then they discussed who would shoulder which responsibilities. They wrapped up their session by asking a series of questions.

Is the list of responsibilities complete?

Do you get frustrated when a procedure or process isn't complete and then comes back to cause difficulties? You can avoid that situation by taking the time to make sure your list of each partner's responsibilities is thorough and complete.

Have all the subtasks for each responsibility been identified?

When establishing a partnership, avoid the informal attitude. Be sure to identify all the tasks for each responsibility. If responsibilities constitute your road map, then the tasks you identify are your street directory. Don't leave your office without them.

Has each responsibility been assigned to someone?

Double-check your list to ensure that either your name or your partner's name appears beside each responsibility. Don't let the excitement of getting your partnership up and running distract you from this essential task.

Has a time frame been established?

Be sure you and your partner agree to a specific time frame that lists all of your tasks and when each is scheduled to be completed. This document is the equivalent of your partnerships' marching orders.

Have effective communications been established?

Finally, have you set up a system to communicate with each other? You should have a plan to let each other know when you have completed a major task. This ensures that you're not working in the dark and that problems don't arise or get out of hand.

Catherine is the type of person who isn't bashful about celebrating success. She does this frequently with her laboratory technicians, and she's taken the initiative to ensure that Dr. Davis doesn't overlook this important phase of the partners' activities.

Celebrate milestones

Catherine wants to celebrate each milestone. It can be as minor as a joint memo to staff, but she wants every accomplishment recognized in some fashion.

Celebrate goals

Catherine insists that they need to celebrate when their common goal is reached. She suggests lunch with members of each partner's staff as part of the celebration.

Can you relate to Catherine's desire to celebrate success? Celebrations can strengthen bonds in a partnership and serve notice to others that the partners achieved a success worthy of commemoration.

The partnerships you establish can be just as productive as the one enjoyed by the Wright brothers. In this topic, you learned about three primary methods for establishing the productive partnerships that will contribute to your success. These methods are:

- identifying common goals,
- establishing the responsibilities of each partner,
- recognizing the need to celebrate accomplishments.

DEALING EFFECTIVELY WITH OPPOSITION

Dealing effectively with opposition

"We have met the enemy and he is us." --Walt Kelley, American cartoonist

Question

Are you your own worst enemy? Do your actions sometimes cause or contribute to opposition in the workplace? When you face opposition, could you use an effective way to deal with it?

Think back to a recent workplace conflict in which you faced opposition. How did you deal with it?

Options:

1. inappropriate
2. undecided
3. appropriate

Answer

Option 1: Self-examination is necessary for you to determine whether you're effective in confronting and coping with opposition rather than increasing it.

Option 2: Honest self-examination is necessary for you to determine whether you're effective in confronting and coping with opposition rather than increasing it.

Option 3: Honest self-examination is necessary for you to determine whether you're effective in confronting and coping with opposition rather than increasing it.

If you desire to do so, you can deal with those who disagree with you. In this topic, you'll learn methods for dealing effectively with opposition in the workplace:

- Identify why opposition exists.
- Understand others' issues.
- Pursue everyone's best interests.

When you identify why opposition exists, you put yourself in a position to follow through and deal with it, in whatever form it takes.

Carrie, an account supervisor, and Matt, a manager in a heavy-equipment manufacturing plant, discussed Matt's opposition to a procedure.

Carrie: Matt, I don't understand your opposition to the new production reporting requirements.

Matt: It adds a lot of additional paperwork to my already busy schedule and to the floor supervisors' schedules as well.

Carrie: You're saying it's additional work, yet you were already reporting most of the data under the old requirements. How much more work do you think you're doing?

Matt: There's definitely more data to collect. It's also a new format that we have to learn, and I didn't see anything wrong with the old format.

Carrie: The old format didn't allow us to capture data on a weekly basis. We now need that to meet the reporting requirements under our contract with the federal government. I would be happy to provide training on the form if that would be helpful.

Matt: Actually, I think we all understand the form now. It just seemed like additional work for no real reason. I'm glad you told me why we're collecting the additional information.

Carrie: Good. I realize I should have told you that at first. That's my mistake. Do you want to pass that reason on to your floor supervisors, or would you like me to come to your next meeting and do that?

Matt: Why don't you come and present the reason? The floor supervisors would see that as a good gesture, and it would help them see that we're one big team dealing with contract requirements.

Carrie and Matt were both satisfied by the end of their conversation, and Matt's stance against the revised reporting requirements had changed. In identifying why Matt disagreed with the requirements, Carrie asked Matt why he was opposed, listened to his response, and then presented her views. This method allowed Carrie to understand the reasons behind Matt's opposition and to effectively address them.

Glenn is using a second method of dealing with opposition: understanding others' issues. Glenn, a writer for a large advertising agency, finds the agency's artists sometimes disagree with his ideas for an ad campaign. Glenn realizes that to deal with their opposition, he needs to understand the artists' issues.

Method 1

"I'm very careful to be objective and avoid any personal issues or disagreements. That keeps the discussion on a professional level when I need to talk about opposition to my ideas or approach it with one of the artists."

Method 2

"My approach is to ask the artist a lot of specific questions to understand her opposition. I want to know exactly what issue the artist has. What's the problem from her viewpoint? For example, does she disagree with my concept, or is it too difficult to implement?"

Method 3

"I always try to brainstorm ideas for resolving the artist's opposition to my approach. Once we understand each other's viewpoints, how can we move forward to achieve a win-win situation for both of us and for the client account? That's the important question."

Method 4

"I want to understand what the impact is on the artist if I don't change my opinion. Is the amount of work I'm asking for causing her opposition? Is it the difficulty of the work? My understanding helps us continue working well together."

If you can understand the viewpoints of others, you'll also understand their issues, which will allow you to deal effectively with opposition.

Pursuing everyone's best interests is the third method you should employ to deal with opposition. Gina, a branch manager for a large bank, was recently involved in two situations where she faced opposition. Each resulted in a different outcome because of Gina's interests.

Response 1

"I said yes--let's resolve this. It was in my interest to overcome the vice president's opposition to my proposal for greater branch control of personnel issues."

Assertive Communication

Response 2
"I said no--let's drop this. It wasn't in anyone's best interest for the discussion to continue. I had invested little in the issue and didn't care strongly about the outcome."

Gina realized that in most situations where disagreement exists, there's a choice of either dealing with the opposition or deciding to drop the issue. The choice will depend on her interests and how she can best pursue them.

Gina reached a rational decision--a yes-or-no decision--because she'd already identified why the opposition existed, and she understood the issues. How can you take a similar approach to dealing with opposition in the workplace?

Question
Opposition is less of a problem for you when you know the right approach to confront it. Which are methods for dealing effectively with opposition in the workplace?

Options:
1. avoiding conflict of interests
2. pursuing everyone's best interests
3. identifying why opposition exists
4. identifying opponents' weaknesses
5. understanding others' issues

Answer
Actually, dealing with opposition involves pursuing your own interests after identifying why opposition exists and what the other person's issues are.

Option 1: This is an incorrect choice. In order to deal effectively with opposition, you have to confront it by trying to understand why it exists, not avoid it. This allows you to deal with it and move on.

Option 2: This is a correct choice. In choosing to pursue everyone's best interests, you focus everyone's energies on issues that really matter instead of issues where the outcome really isn't important overall.

Option 3: This choice is correct. In identifying why opposition exists, you discover ways you can address the opposition. By investigating, your questions will reveal answers that lead to solutions and keep things moving.

Option 4: This choice is incorrect. You need to understand others' reasons for opposition so you can effectively address them to resolve conflict. Identifying weaknesses does not take others' concerns into account.

Option 5: This is a correct choice. You should seek to understand where others stand and how they see a decision, or failure to make a decision, as impacting their work. Once all sides are understood, a solution can be reached.

In this topic, you learned that dealing effectively with opposition requires you to identify why opposition exists and to understand the opponents' issues as well as decide how best to pursue your interests.

Developing assertiveness from the inside out puts you in charge of your professional style--developing your style today and planning how to best use it in the future. If you want to successfully develop the assertive style you've dreamed of having, you have to take a positive approach by using self-development and interactive strategies. This course provided some steps and methods for using these strategies to achieve your desired professional assertive style.

REFERENCES

References
- **13 Fatal Errors Managers Make and How You Can Avoid Them** - 1995, Brown, W. Steven, Berkley Books
- **Managing Assertively** - 1995, Burley-Allen, Madelyn, John Wiley & Sons
- **The 7 Habits of Highly Effective People** - 1990, Covey, Stephen R., Simon & Schuster
- **1001 Ways to Reward Employees** - 1994, Nelson, Bob, Workman Publishing
- **Leadership Secrets of Attila the Hun** - 1991, Roberts, Wess, Warner Books
- **Getting Together: Building Relationships as We Negotiate** - 1988, Fisher, Roger, and Scott Brown, Penguin Books
- **Getting to Yes: Negotiating Agreement without Giving In** - 1985, Fisher, Roger, and William Ury, Penguin Books

GLOSSARY

Glossary

A

aggressive - Behavior seen by others as hostile or destructive when used inappropriately. Aggressive behavior may be appropriate when dealing with an emergency or with very difficult subordinates.

assertive - Behavior seen by others as forceful and positive.

C

constructive criticism - Identifying a specific, current issue and giving critical feedback that contains suggestions or a plan of action for improving the behaviors or actions that received criticism.

F

feedback - Commentary given to a co-worker about his or her behavior or actions.

M

management style - The way you conduct yourself in providing feedback and constructive criticism to subordinates. Styles range from passive to assertive to aggressive.

manager - Someone who exercises executive authority to manage and control business activities.

P

passive - Behavior seen by others as overly submissive. Confrontation is avoided even when it is called for by the situation at hand.

positive reinforcement - Praise intended to cause a person to repeat a desirable action.

professional style - The way you conduct yourself as you interact with co-workers and deal with them in the workplace.

S

supervisor - Someone you report to at work who is responsible for your work product and workplace activities and behavior.

www.ingramcontent.com/pod-product-compliance
Lightning Source LLC
Chambersburg PA
CBHW020914180526
45163CB00007B/2732